# ONE SOUL
# ONE MIND

# ONE SOUL
# ONE MIND

## A Study of Homosexuality
## and Gender Identity

# G. M. WALSER

BROWN BOOKS
PUBLISHING GROUP

© 2016 G. M. Walser

*One Soul/One Mind*
*A Study of Homosexuality and Gender Identity*

Brown Books Publishing Group
16250 Knoll Trail Drive, Suite 205
Dallas, Texas 75248
www.BrownBooks.com
(972) 381-0009
A New Era in Publishing®

ISBN 978-1-61254-889-0
LCCN 2015956066

Printed in the United States
10 9 8 7 6 5 4 3 2 1

For more information or to contact the author, please go to
www.OnesSoulOneMind.com.

I dedicate this book to all the LGBTQ children and adults around the world.

# TABLE OF CONTENTS

# ACKNOWLEDGMENTS

First and foremost, I want to thank God for the intuition, the inspiration, and the courage to face reality with which He blessed me, for all the doors that He has opened for me throughout my life's journey, and for directing me to find the answers to all my questions while searching for the truth. I also want to thank my two daughters for their contributions directly and indirectly to this book. Last but not least, I want to thank Jeff Putnam, who has been pivotal in helping me to write, organize, and arrange my thoughts and experiences for my book, as well as the people of Brown Books Publishing Group for their vital contribution in shaping and making this project—my dream—come to life.

# INTRODUCTION

Writing this book was hard for me because I was afraid of hurting people I loved. Also, my clients from my beauty salon and my cosmetic company had, over the years, become like family to me. I couldn't have survived without their many kindnesses. Yet I quickly discovered that no one I had known wanted his or her name to be used in a book about homosexuality.

Still, for well over twenty years, I have been gathering evidence that I was responsible for my second daughter's gender differences and that many parents, without knowing it, are responsible for gender differences in their own children. What were only hunches or intuition in the beginning were supported by documented cases the more I read and studied the problem.

Needless to say, I could never change any minds by saying, "You're wrong; I know better." All I can say is that my intuition must have come from God through prayer. And I now realize that my daughter is the source of all the insights that have changed my life for the better: all the peace and happiness that have come to me in truly knowing who she is, how she feels about herself, and how much she has loved me. She thanks me now for the way I have always shown my love, and I thank her for all the love and support she has shown me in my struggle to survive.

Yes, I would very much like to be able to help stop the persecution of certain people for expressing their God-given feelings and traits of character. And I realize now that this persecution has a long history. Perhaps we're seeing less of it now; it could be that more people are looking the other way. Anyway, if I can change some minds by telling my story, good. At least I will no longer be plagued by guilt for keeping silent.

In this country, we have had a wave of events that have been dramatic and painful for many people. We have heard of or seen suicide among young people due to bullying and discrimination, all because they were gay. These are young homosexual people in crisis. The percentage of homeless LGBT (lesbian, gay, bisexual, transgender) youth in this country is too high (40 percent of the homeless youth served by agencies were identified as LGBT [Gates and Newport 2012]). Young people with gender issues are discriminated against, stigmatized, and very often abandoned and rejected by their own parents and families, which adds to their emotional stress and to the many challenges they face. Generally, people with gender identity differences are avoided. Many people want to stay away from them because of the notion that LBGTQ (lesbian, bisexual, gay, transgender, queer) is contagious, suggestive, or immoral. However, there is no danger in being around homosexuals or people with gender identity differences; we are the way we are, and we cannot change what God instilled in each of us.

These facts, experiences, and attitudes have motivated me to write this book. It is shameful to know that much of the suffering in this world is due to a lack of knowledge. Knowledge is the secret to understanding creation. We suffer and cause others to suffer unnecessarily not only because of ignorance but also because of our lack of compassion. My motivation in writing this book about gender identity and homosexuality in general is to promote respect and empathy for people who are at risk for violence, abuse, and exploitation. In addition, I want people to understand that there is nothing these children and adults have done to be this way. We are all born with some kind of limitation—mental, physical, or spiritual. Sexual orientation is not a choice for them; instead, that is who they are from birth, and even in utero.

We are created as whole beings, equipped with a system that operates at all levels: mind, body, and spirit. The mind is energy that has immeasurable power, divided into the conscious and subconscious (unconscious) minds. The conscious mind is our thinking mind, and the subconscious mind stores and collects emotions. The body consists of organs, systems, and cells. The spirit is the essence of life, the part of us attributed to our connection with God. Consequently, we cannot separate the mind, body, and spirit from each other; they are intrinsically connected.

I feel very fortunate to have been given so much by the people I've encountered on my path through life—not just the people who knew me personally, but the authors of all the books I read—who helped me to become the person I wanted to be, united in mind, body, and spirit. The path to understanding my daughter taught me the most important things I needed to know about myself. My deepest desire is to spark a meeting of the minds that control our beliefs, feelings, and attitudes about gender identity so that we may become of "one soul/one mind."

# DEFINITIONS

Gender identity disorder (GID) is classified as a medical condition and defined as:

> A conflict between a person's physical gender and the gender he or she identifies as. For example, a person identified as a boy may actually feel and act like a girl. The person is very uncomfortable with the gender they were born. (A.D.A.M., Inc. 2015)

From a social perspective, the ideas of confusion, turmoil, unrest, and chaos are also associated with the word "disorder." While these reactions may describe the lives of individuals born with gender differences, they are caused by the behavior and attitudes of people they come in contact with. When those who are misinformed—people who don't know the cause or root of homosexual behaviors—react with disapproval, anger, and hatred, they promote and perpetuate the idea of a gender identity conflict as a "disorder." Other widely used terms related to homosexuality, such as "lesbian," "gay," "bisexual," "transgender," and "queer," are also too harsh when describing our children because they are associated with both abnormality and immorality in our society. Fortunately, my daughter sees herself as a normal human being classified with an interpretation of gender identity.

GID may be caused by "hormones in the womb, genes, [and/or] social and environmental factors (such as parenting)." The disorder may occur in both children and adults. Although symptoms vary with age and social environment, they include: disgust with one's own genitals, rejection by peers, loneliness, the desire to live as a person of the opposite sex, depression, anxiety, cross-dressing, and withdrawal from social interaction. The feeling of being the "wrong" gender must last at least two years before the diagnosis can be made. GID is not necessarily the same as homosexuality. Persons with GID "may act and present themselves as members of the opposite sex"; choice of sexual partners [the same sex or the opposite sex], mannerisms, behavior, dress, and self-concept may be affected (A.D.A.M., Inc. 2015).

Although the term GID has been updated to *gender dysphoria*, the treatments remain the same: early diagnosis; individual and family therapy; a supportive environment at home and in school (A.D.A.M., Inc. 2015). However, in my experience, diagnosis and treatment may be unnecessary if you have an understanding of what causes the gender differences in the first place. If homosexuality and gender identity or dysphoria weren't so stigmatized and people were more accepting of other human imperfections, LGBTQ corrections would not be necessary. All kinds of research has been funded to explore the behavior of young people who have problems. Reputations have been made, books have been written, and innovative therapeutic approaches have been devised by people who spent years of their own lives working on gender identity conflicts. Wouldn't it be better to support research that might enable people to prevent the problem in the first place?

# PART 1

## MIND

The mind, body, and spirit are connected. From my experience and research, I have come to understand that physical factors influence the mind and spirit, and mental and spiritual factors influence the body. I practice a holistic approach to my overall health, and my goal is for you to see how these human aspects are interrelated. Since the conscious mind controls our thoughts and emotions, I will begin with glimpses into the most formative moments of my life, starting with my childhood and adolescence in Ecuador and my later move to the United States.

# ONE
## My Childhood in Ecuador

While writing this book, I had to remember and relive years of chaos and fear. On the other hand, it gives me joy to go back to my childhood in Loja, Ecuador—a childhood completely happy in so many ways . . .

I was born in the city of Loja, the musical and cultural capital of Ecuador. I was educated at the private Catholic school La Inmaculada Concepción. My childhood in the city of Loja was full of good memories. At La Inmaculada Concepción, there were plenty of activities throughout the year, such as musical and dramatic plays. I took part in many of the plays, once taking the part of Cinderella. We had a lot of fun.

My parents were good Catholic people, both hard workers and extremely creative. I was the third of eleven children, the oldest of the girls.

When I was sixteen, my parents moved our family to Quito, the capital city of Ecuador, where there were better educational opportunities for us children. I resumed my education at La Providencia, a private Catholic high school.

My dream was to be a painter. I was born with artistic talent, and ever since I can remember, I liked to draw. My favorite subject was literature. I felt as if I was the painter and the poet in my family.

My father was opposed to the idea of me being a painter. He used to tell me to be practical: Painters do not become famous until after they die! You need to do something that will make you a living while you are alive. I respected my father's wishes for reasons I will presently explain. So, it was because of him that I had to choose a career in business.

Above all, my father was my hero, my mentor, and my guide. Being the first and oldest girl in my family gave me a certain kind of advantage or privilege, I think. Besides, my father and I were very much alike.

In my father's family, there were four girls and two boys. He was the oldest boy and only two years old when his young father died. In the early twentieth century, women in my small country of Ecuador did not work outside the home. My grandmother herself was an orphan who had lost both of her parents at the age of eleven. According to my father, they had very wealthy relatives, but they were not too generous to this young widow and her children. My grandmother and her children struggled for a few years.

When my father was seven years old, his godfather, who had a good position at an American gold mine in my country, had an idea of how to help my grandmother. The gold mine company provided housing for their workers. My father was the only one who could work in his young family, doing anything he could: being an errand boy, picking weeds, just anything that a young boy could do. Still, he managed to go to school.

The American employers loved my father, and my father loved them, too. Since my father had lost his father at such a young age, he looked up to the Americans, who had a lot to do with his upbringing. He remembered playing baseball with them. I did not know what baseball was at the time. He always spoke very highly of his American friends and told me that they were all good people. I believe that was one of the reasons I married Americans twice, thinking that they were all good people as my father had always said.

My father was a man of integrity and extremely compassionate to people in need. He worked for the American company for twenty-five years, retiring at the age of thirty-two. Before he retired, he was the head of the construction department, one of the youngest ever to fill that position and one of the youngest retirees. From my father's work, I learned the meaning of ethics, integrity, and survival skills.

Once my father retired from the gold mine company, he went back to his mother's hometown of Loja. He started a lumberyard business and did very well. Being among the oldest in my family, I have good, vivid memories about the sawmill and the fun we had playing with sawdust.

After the move to Quito, he opened up an automobile parts business like the rest of the males in his family, and he worked very hard until he retired from that business at age seventy-five.

One thing that has stuck in my mind about my father was his hunger for knowledge. He was self-educated, since he did not have the opportunity to seek higher education. In my country, if you don't have the money, you do not have the chance for an education.

My father did not smoke or drink, and he was an example of honesty and responsibility, especially with his wife and children. To me, my father was an extraordinary and remarkable man.

# TWO
## My Education

During the summer of 1963, while I was still going through high school, I worked for the government at the Treasury Department. The summer of 1964, I worked again for the government at the Agriculture and Livestock Department as a secretary. In 1965, I graduated as a public accountant in business administration. (I had the hardest time with algebra and trigonometry; I hated these subjects, but I did it.)

In 1967, I enrolled in the School of Linguistics at the Catholic University in Quito. In 1968, while a student at Pontifical Catholic University, I had the opportunity to go to Trinity Catholic College in Washington, DC, for an international intensive English summer course. There were five students from Ecuador. This was an unbelievable experience. I got to meet young people from many, many countries, and this was also my first time in the United States.

One experience stands out. I was twenty-two years old, and some of the students were younger. After a long week of eight-hour days studying the English language, all of the students were ready to get out of school and go explore the city. On weekends, the two other Ecuadorian girls and I would go to see the main tourist attractions. We went on a White House tour; we also visited Capitol Hill, the Lincoln Memorial, Washington National Cathedral, the National Monument, the Smithsonian Museum, and Arlington National Cemetery, among other places of interest.

Before I tell this unpleasant, but funny, true story, I want to point out that this was in the 1960s. My country, especially Quito, had been invaded by hippies from many countries and especially from the United States. Most, or maybe all of them, were there for the easy access to drugs. Their looks were very much those of homeless people. This is the reason we were such willing participants in what happened that afternoon.

It was a Sunday; my two Ecuadorian friends and I went to the Smithsonian Museum. We left the museum at about three in the afternoon. We walked several blocks then began to feel hungry and started looking for a place to eat. I don't remember how far we walked or in which direction as we tried to find a place with food.

This was 1968, and hippies were everywhere. Finally, we saw what looked like a restaurant; there were a lot of hippies in line. We didn't think twice. The food smelled good. It was almost four in the afternoon, and we were starving. We got in line. When we got our food, we sat down to eat. Suddenly, I noticed that a guy across from me at the table was smiling and had no teeth. Most of the people there were staring at us.

We kept eating; the food was good. (There is never bad food when one is starving.) We got up and went to pay. The lady who was serving, very sweetly and with a grin on her face, said, "There is no charge. Here, we feed the homeless."

Although we were all dressed up, we felt ashamed and embarrassed. We were in shock! You see, in my country, we do not have social programs or these types of places, only restaurants where you have to pay your way. When we left, we laughed all the way back to the college. We told our teachers and the nuns, and they laughed, too. They thought that this was the funniest thing that could happen to anybody. I still laugh when I remember this event. How awful it was!

Unfortunately, today in Ecuador, nearly 40 percent of Ecuadoreans live in poverty; another 13 percent live in extreme poverty (Seelke 2008). Nevertheless, Ecuador's natural resources include petroleum, bananas, cut flowers, and shrimp, with exports totaling $25.48 billion (estimated in 2013).

This South American country has made enormous social investments over the past eight years of the Correa government. Recently, the Ecuadorean Natural Secretary for Planning and Development announced that between 2007 and 2014, more than 1.5 million people had been lifted out of poverty. "The model of government has radically changed," said Secretary Pabel Muñoz (teleSUR 2015). No doubt things have changed in my country, but the Ecuadorean people still have to tolerate corruption at all levels of government.

At the end of 1968, I opened my first business. I was twenty-three years old. This business—Agencias y Servicios, Quito, Ecuador—was an employment agency for secretaries, public accountants, bilingual secretaries, etc. After my first daughter was born, I had to stay home for a while to be available for her at any time. When I felt the time was right, after this period at home with my baby, I began working as a teacher for Casa de la Cultura Ecuatoriana Instituto de Manualidades y Artesanias Populares. Although I was younger than all of my students, I taught there from 1971 to 1972. Then, because of the flexibility of the schedule, I started to work for my father's automobile parts business, keeping books; all throughout this time, we had a live-in maid to take care of my daughter. From 1974 to 1976, I worked for the government again, this time at the Industry, Commerce, and Integration Department. Our office dealt with foreign investors, and I worked as a bilingual translator/secretary.

One of the new investors to move to our country was a German gentleman named Mr. Backhaus (name has been changed). He was very pleased that I was able to expedite the documentation and paper-work for his investments in Ecuador. He had to come to my office several times to sign documents. We got acquainted and began to talk. He was a chemical engineer, and he talked about cosmetics manufacturing. I was very interested in this field, so he said he could sell me some formulas and teach me how to manufacture products with them. I agreed with his terms, and on July 3, 1974, I bought his formulas. Since I have always been very artistic, I already knew how to make cosmetics, and I already had experience in running a business, so I thought, *why not?*

In 1976, I started my own cosmetics company. As manager/owner of a cosmetics firm, I worked very hard during the first years because I had acquired several loans to start my business. At the end of the first year, I was able to pay back all the money that I had borrowed. I was also working hard to support my first child.

While working for the government during the year before I started my company, I had the opportunity to go to Rio de Janeiro, Brazil, to take a look at the cosmetics business. I also had the chance to visit several cosmetics companies in São Paulo, Brazil. With this experience and all the new ideas I had acquired from it, I was ready for my new business endeavor.

My business was doing very well, and I was also teaching private lessons in handicrafts. I was a very busy person!

# THREE
## The Meal That Changed My Life

One day in 1980, I went to eat with a friend I hadn't seen in years, a schoolmate from my hometown of Loja. We went to a very popular restaurant in Quito. While we were chatting and catching up with life's events, I noticed through a mirror that this young American was looking intently at me—staring at me, in fact. He acted as if he had never seen anybody so pretty. (I later learned that this was what he did with every woman.)

He was eating with an older American man. I told my friend what was happening, and we continued talking. After about fifteen minutes or so, the older man came to our table. He spoke Spanish very well. I do not remember what he asked us, but he seemed very nice and polite. After a while, his young friend joined us. He did not speak Spanish, but I spoke enough English to start a conversation. The older American man had already asked my friend for my phone number, which he intended to give to his young friend. I did not know that until a week later, when this young man called me for the first time.

This young American man was well dressed, very nice looking, and polite. He started calling me every day. After a month of dating, he asked me to marry him. It was too soon, I thought; I did not know him well enough. Later, I introduced him to my family and friends; everybody liked him except my mother, who said that there was something about him she did not like. In fact, she said to me, "There's something about his eyes. He looks like a crazy man."

Like most young people, I did not listen to my mother. I was a single mother at the time, and my daughter was ten years old.

The man had told me that he was an engineer for Texaco and was working for them in Ecuador. He also told me that he had a five-year contract with that company and that he intended to stay. I thought that if he stayed in Ecuador for five years, maybe he would stay for good. He told me that his parents lived in a big house in Texas. I believed everything he told me.

Three months later, I agreed to marry him. We traveled to the States to get married, and we were supposed to go back to Ecuador, but he had lied to me. He did not have a five-year contract. His parents did not have a big house; they had a very small house, and in the back of this house was a travel trailer that was going to be my residence. I was extremely disappointed and upset and knew that I had been taken in by a liar.

My husband was the only child. His father was a very nice man, and he liked us a lot. His mother was extremely strange and displayed a lot of odd behavior. My then-father-in-law was around for a year and a half, more or less, before he became ill with cancer and died during the second year of my marriage.

Three months after we got married, I found on top of my husband's night table an envelope addressed to my then-mother-in-law. It was open, so I got curious and read it. To my surprise, it was a response to my mother-in-law from a company that sold cosmetic containers. I immediately realized that this man and his mother were in a scheme to put me to work. I confronted my husband and told him that that would not happen. I would do it when I was ready and on my own terms. I also told him that I had realized now why he married me. I wanted to go back home right away, but he threw a fit and threatened me. Also, my pride was making it difficult for me to go home and admit that I had made such a foolish mistake.

In the following years, I found out more lies. My husband was a school dropout, not an engineer. He was also a womanizer, a drug user, and many more things that were unacceptable by my standards.

After six months of living in that trailer, I felt like a bird in a cage. I demanded that we get a house, or I would go back to my country. I had money from my business account from home. We used that money as a down payment when we found a home in Guthrie, a small town not that far from his parents' home in the Texas Panhandle. I felt I had come to the end of the world. Instead of trees, there were "tumbleweeds" blowing across the flat and dusty plains. This was the life I had chosen for myself. This was where my dreams had come to die.

Thank goodness, this man was gone a lot of the time, mostly to jobs overseas. I think that out of the five years I was married to him, we spent at the most one and a half or two years together. At the end of the fifth year, I told my oldest daughter, "The next time he goes overseas, we will go back home to Ecuador."

At that time, I was not feeling well and did not know what was wrong with me. At the same time, I was going to a community college, taking an English refresher course. A lady in my class was pregnant, and I told her that I was glad that she, not I, was the one who was pregnant, not knowing that I had been pregnant for two months already. When I continued to feel unwell, I asked my friend from college to go with me to her doctor. I thought my change of life was beginning or even some form of cancer.

When the doctor was through examining me, he told me that I was pregnant. This was a blow. I felt I was trapped for good in this terrible marriage. I cried all the way back home.

As for my pregnancy: physically, I was very healthy, but emotion-ally, I was not so well. I was thirty-nine years old and would be forty when this baby was born. At the time, I felt very old to be pregnant again, and, of course, I was in the midst of a failing marriage.

After I accepted the fact that I was pregnant, my husband, the father-to-be (a man who had never, to his knowledge, had a child before), seemed happy. I thought maybe this child would change his ways. From the beginning of my pregnancy, he had wanted his child to be a boy.

By the second month of my pregnancy, I had to have a sonogram to determine how far along I was pregnant. My gynecologist told me that he could not determine the gender of the baby at that time. He recommended an amniocentesis because of my age, but I felt there was too much risk involved, so I didn't have it done. Seven months later, I delivered a healthy little girl.

# FOUR
## My Marriage Crisis

After five years of marriage, and only weeks before our first baby, my husband had begun staying in his pickup for a while before coming into the house after he had been out. About the third time I saw him out there, I realized he was reading something. If I came out of the house to greet him, he would hide what he was reading under the car seat. This happened several times before I saw my chance to see what he was up to.

While he was napping inside one evening, I quietly went out to his pickup to see what he'd been reading. Aha! It was one of those so-called men's magazines with pictures of naked women. I don't know what I was expecting, but I remember a moment of relief. At least he'd had enough respect for me to hide it. The reality was that I'd been disappointed by him so many times in our marriage, it was a comparatively minor betrayal for him to be looking at pictures of other women.

I'd kept myself well, but I would be forty years old when the new baby came into our lives. My fifteen-year-old daughter was living with us, and she was the main reason I'd stayed in Texas after finding out about my husband's problems with drugs and other women. For a long time, I'd maintained a slender thread of hope that he would mend his ways when the new baby arrived, that he'd take seriously the duties of fatherhood even if he could never manage more than a minimum standard of decency as a husband.

When I looked under the seat of his truck, I found an article that began where the pages of the magazine had been folded back, and I began to read it. The article gave advice to readers on "how to impress a woman." *What in the world . . .?*

The article instructed a man who is driving an expensive car to leave his lights on when he goes into a bar. That way, when there's an announcement about the black Cadillac with its lights on, all the women who had gone to the bar that night to meet men would know that the man who answered the public announcement was the driver of an expensive car. Another tip was to open one's wallet and flash as many credit cards as possible when the credit card holder dropped down. Pathetic as all this was, I didn't call him on it—yet.

Closer still to my due date, my husband began applying for all kinds of credit cards he didn't need. He told me, "You should have them, too!"

"I know why you're doing this," I told him, but he wasn't yet able to put two and two together.

Two weeks after the birth of our baby, he left our home in Guthrie, in the panhandle of West Texas, to take a job in Brownsville, and I didn't hear from him or get any support from him for a long while. Three months later, he came home for Christmas, and when I went to pick him up at the airport, he was drunk. I was in shock and scared.

The next day, he decided to go buy a new vehicle. I was driving a nice Cadillac at the time, and it was only two years old. We didn't need a new car! But he insisted and said that it was for the baby: "The baby's first car," as he put it.

*How ridiculous and dumb this man is*, I thought, *to be trading in my good car for a brand-new Cadillac that we don't need and can't afford!* I was more than a little upset that evening as we drove the new car home. I couldn't get over his stupidity, but what could I do, if he was going to be paying for it?

Two days later, right after Christmas of 1985, he went back to Brownsville, but, before he left, he took five thousand dollars from the savings account that I had been maintaining. He was going to invest in a business that was supposed to make us a lot of money.

About two weeks after my baby was born, my husband had gone to work in Brownsville. A few days after he left, I was notified by an employee of an insurance company of a transaction that had caused the company concern. When my baby was only three days old, my husband (not yet my ex-husband) had taken out a $50,000 life insurance policy on our baby daughter. They considered this highly unusual, and I suppose it was, but I felt blessed with the information because it enabled me to be more vigilant and prevent any harm from coming to the daughter that he seemed not to care about. (Later, I told my attorney about this, and through a court order, the baby's father was restrained from being alone with my child.)

My husband had caused trouble and cheated the whole time that we'd been married, but I just hadn't been able to prove it yet. This time, he wasn't so lucky. I'd had a credit card since I'd been running my cosmetics business in Ecuador. When I married this man, I'd added his name to my account. So it happened that one day in February 1986 I got a bill from the credit card company. At the time, bills would come with copies of a receipt from each of the businesses from which a purchase had been made. One of the receipts was for over six hundred dollars. It had a signature that was not his in what appeared to be a woman's handwriting.

I immediately thought, *Maybe the credit card has been stolen from him.* Otherwise, how could he expect me to pay his expenses when he wasn't sending me any money? The receipt was from a mechanic's shop and had their address and phone number. I decided to call and try to find out who was using the card. I told the mechanic who answered the phone that this was my credit card and that the transaction had seemed suspicious. He was very nice and told me that a pickup had been repaired. He gave me the description of a vehicle that exactly matched my husband's. He said that a woman had come to pick it up. Right away, I asked if she had given him a number or an address. The mechanic kindly gave me her address and phone number.

That evening, I called the number, and a very shy young girl who spoke almost no English answered. I asked her in Spanish if she knew my husband, and when she said she did, I asked her if he was there. In Spanish, she told me, "No, he's not here yet, but he comes home around seven in the evening." She told me she was their maid. I thanked her and waited until seven; then I called again.

A woman answered the phone this time. I told her who I was; she did not seem in the least disturbed. I asked her to put my husband on the line, and she went to get him. When he got on the phone, I told him I knew what was going on and that he would be hearing from me.

The next day, I called and talked to the maid. She was scared when I told her who I was.

"If my parents find out I'm working for people like that, they won't let me work anymore."

"Yes, but don't you think it would make them happy if you helped me?" I replied.

She agreed that it would and gave me all the information I needed. Three days later, I filed for divorce.

Meanwhile, I didn't know what I was going to do. I couldn't sleep at night, wondering how I was going to provide for my children. What was going to happen to us? The night seemed to last for an eternity. How could I sleep while I was enraged by this man's actions? How could he have a woman with a maid when his only child was not getting any support?

I needed to be a detective. The next day, I called the girl in Browns-ville again and asked her some more questions. She told me everything. The woman was a blonde American. She was in the process of getting a divorce, and she had a daughter who was about six years old. She was still married to a businessman, a Mexican American. I asked if she knew his name, and she did, so I got his name. She didn't know his phone number, but I told her, "I can get that."

But it wasn't going to be easy. He had a very common Hispan-ic surname—I'll call him Juan Martinez to protect his identity. The information operator in Brownsville told me that there were a page and a half of men with the man's real name. In accordance with the telephone company's rules, she could only give me the numbers six at a time. I agreed and got the first six numbers. Before calling any of them, I prayed. I knew I would have to have God's help to find my way out of the mess I was in. I knew God would have to be my "husband" and the "father" of my children.

I intended to rely on God completely for the courage I would need in the months and years ahead. God would give me inspiration and help me find the right ideas and actions to provide for my little family here in this foreign country, in this little town in the West Texas Panhandle that had seemed to me, right from the first, to be the end of the world. This place was different from everything I had known growing up. My native country was full of mountains and streams and valleys lush with plants of all kinds. The headwaters of the Amazon began on the east-ern slopes of the Andes, and the jungle was already dense in Ecuador. But I had grown up in Loja, which was surrounded by beautiful valleys, and then in Quito, a modern city, during my college years. I simply didn't belong where I found myself now. With God's help, however, I would put down roots and, in so doing, honor the wishes of my eldest daughter, who had always asked so little of me and helped so much. These days, she was an enormous help looking after the needs of my new baby, a beautiful, vigorous child full of healthy curiosity.

As I went down my list, I said to each respondent in turn, "I'm looking for Juan Martinez, the husband of Dina Martinez." With the third call I made, the man who answered said, "Yes, that's me."

I told him I was the wife of the man his wife was living with. He didn't seem terribly surprised, but I could tell he was genuinely happy to assist me. Here we were, two people experiencing the same kind of pain. He had filed for divorce because of his wife's betrayal, and I was divorcing my husband for the same reason. From the moment we spoke on the phone, we became close allies. He gave me all the information I needed at the time. In return, I gave *him* all the information that he needed.

Juan Martinez would call regularly to let me know what was going on. In passing, he told me that he had a well-established business in Brownsville and its suburbs. He imported peppers of all kinds from Mexico and sold them to Mexican restaurants and grocery stores in the area. He told me that Dina wanted half the business.

"Nobody is going to buy anything from her," he went on to say. "All the restaurant owners are my clients and friends." He also mentioned that, prior to filing for divorce, he had bought his wife a new Cadillac, but he had stopped making the payments. He also said that my husband had told Dina that he was an oilman and that he gave me a new Cadillac every year for Christmas. (By the way, he'd never made the first payments; I had been stuck with the car and the payments.)

In the meantime, my soon-to-be ex-husband would call to harass me and make trouble. He wouldn't ask about the baby, but he would ask how the Cadillac was running. I knew he was trying to impress someone, so I would say, "What Cadillac are you talking about? I don't know anything about a Cadillac."

When I asked what he was doing with the five thousand dollars he had taken, he said he had invested in "the onion business." He still had no idea that I was getting information from Dina's soon-to-be ex-husband.

A month after my last phone contact with my husband, Mr. Martinez called to tell me that Dina and my husband had bought a truckload of jalapeño peppers to sell. Three days later, they had a truck full of rotten peppers. Nobody wanted to do business with them. A week later, my husband called. When I answered the phone, I said "Hmm . . . I don't know what's happening, but as soon as I picked up the receiver, there was a terrible smell coming from the phone. It smells like rotten jalapeño peppers!" He didn't say anything and hung up the phone. I had to laugh. To be sure, I was still hurt because of all that had happened, but my husband's behavior struck me as comical.

Mr. Martinez and I stayed in touch. We tried everything we could think of to have a little fun with the situation. Meanwhile, neither of the two lowlifes who were trying to take advantage of us knew what was really happening.

About three months after we had filed for divorce, there was a court hearing, and my husband had to come to the Panhandle. When my lawyer asked him for a physical address, he said, "My girlfriend and I are staying over at my friend's house." I knew which friend it was when he gave the name and address. There was no surprise in where he was staying, but I was shocked to realize that he had brought the woman with him. The only reason he could have done it was to hurt my feelings.

After the court hearing, that same afternoon, a man from Brownsville called me. He turned out to be with the company in Brownsville that was financing Dina's Cadillac. He said he was looking for my husband. Then he said, "I'm not looking for him, really, but for the woman that's with him." He told me that she was five months behind in her car payments, and he was trying to repossess the car. I asked the man who had given him my phone number, and he said, "Her husband, Mr. Martinez." I told him that I just happened to know where they were staying. Would he be good enough to let me know when he got the car?

The next morning was a Saturday, and the repo man called again. He said he couldn't find the two of them at the address I'd given him. Did I have any other ideas about where they might be?

"When did you go to the address I gave you?" I asked.

"Last night. Friday night."

"They probably went out drinking. If you want to catch them in, I'd go early in the morning."

Late Monday morning, the repo man called to let me know that he'd gotten the car. And he told me everything that had happened. He and his repo people had gone there early on Sunday morning. Once they had loaded the car, they had knocked on the door. My husband's friend had opened it, and they had told him what was going on.

When my husband and his girlfriend came out, there was general embarrassment. The repo man said they were looking at each other for answers, but even with very few words, it was all too clear what they were thinking. The woman wanted to know, *If you're so rich, why didn't you pay them what I owe on the car so I can keep it?* My husband was clearly wondering, *If you have so much money, how come they're repossessing your car?*

My husband called on Monday evening, and I heard a softness in his voice that I hadn't heard in quite a while. I told him, "I have the feeling that you want to borrow one of my cars!" There were two cars in the garage because my oldest daughter already had one of her own. All he could say in response was, "I don't know what you are talking about," before he hung up the phone.

He'd gone to his friend's house with his rich girlfriend to impress the friend and his family. Two days later, he and his girlfriend were leaving town in an old truck he had taken from his mother's place without asking. Since his mother didn't know who had taken the old truck, she reported it stolen. After the criminals got back to Brownsville, they split up immediately. My husband moved on to Arizona. The police finally found the old truck, and he was arrested.

I was still too hurt to fall down laughing after all this man had put me through, but it was too funny not to laugh at all. I had tears in my eyes, but, this time, the tears felt good. I still laugh at the memory of how my husband's plans had backfired. I came up with the following moral for the story: when you're reading trash about how to impress people, don't think you're the only idiot who's reading it. It was plain as anything that they'd both read the same kind of article, and they'd both gotten what they deserved.

Juan Martinez and I said goodbye on the phone and had a last laugh together. There was nothing left for us to do. Sherlock Holmes and Dr. Watson were going their separate ways, mission accomplished.

God had been my partner all through this period, helping me to find the strength to do what I had to do. Yet his role in helping me to find my way after my disastrous marriage wasn't over. There were more instances of help from God that were unmistakable to his faithful servant.

On two occasions, I was in urgent need of funds—in the first case, to keep up payments I needed to make in order to stay in school and get the license I needed to go into business for myself with a beauty salon. Miraculously, the money I needed was waiting for me at the mailbox in a plain envelope with my name on it. My ex-husband had tried to make good on some back alimony, perhaps to stay out of jail. I didn't question how he got the money. I never had—I knew all I ever wanted to know about my ex-husband's life.

On the next occasion that I received help from out of the blue, it came when I was up against the wall, trying to make the last mortgage payment on my business. This time, the miracle came in the form of a check from the Child Support Enforcement division of the Texas Attorney General's Office. Again, the amount was just what I needed to keep from having to close my doors.

Still, I felt there had been some mistake, and I called the office that had sent the check. I explained that I was unaware that I had any money coming from them. In fact, during a one-day stretch in jail for nonsupport, my ex-husband had written a pile of checks and backdated them as if to show that he'd been making his payments all along. Then he'd had an acquaintance take the checks to the office that had thrown him in jail until they relented, and then he began to support his child.

The people at the agency told me that there had been no mistake. They had mailed me the money because my ex-husband had overpaid and they had no idea where to find him. I didn't know where to find him, either, but I wasn't going to watch my business go under while I went looking.

There was occasional contact between us, and, at one point, he asked me why I thought I would always have luck on my side. I told him that it wasn't luck I'd had on my side; it was God—simple as that. I'd prayed fervently for guidance every day, and I'd felt the hand of God in all my affairs, including the ugly business of trying to keep my ex-husband out of my life as much as possible.

He sneered at the thought that I could have God's help. He couldn't have known at the time that the greatest gift God had ever bestowed on me had nothing to do with money. It had to do with the safety of my child—his biological child—who was in danger of coming to harm from him.

* * *

Now it's time to evict this man from the book I'm writing about my life and my second daughter to focus on the way that knowledge, intuition, and faith—mind, body, and spirit—have worked together to help me find the right path. Despite the suffering that my marriage brought me, I never stopped looking to God for help and thanking him when I received it. And I was never ungrateful for the great blessing of my two daughters and especially of my baby girl. I was grateful not only for the person my baby turned out to be but for the things I learned from her that changed my life.

Still, there's no way I can turn away from the events that led me to Guthrie, Texas, where I was able to give my two children a fighting chance to make a good life for themselves. Both are now successful, and I, too, was successful beyond my wildest dreams—or at least beyond anything I could have imagined happening when I was lying awake at night, wondering how I could manage alone in a foreign country where I didn't speak the language well enough to go into business doing what I could do best and where I didn't have enough money to make such a start in any case.

I feel better now about telling the story of how I got to the panhandle of Texas, and I have learned what I had to know to make a success of my life there.

# FIVE
## Abandoned by My Husband with a New Baby

With my husband gone, there would be no checks in the mail this time. The writing may have been on the wall from that moment, but the full realization of what I was up against didn't sink in for a further six weeks, when credit card statements tipped me off that he had once again lied to me and was, in fact, living with another woman, as I've already related.

The year was 1986, and a lot of things about my life were about to change.

As soon as I found out that my husband was living with another woman, I had gone to see a priest from the only Catholic church in our area. I needed direction about what I should do about my life now that my husband was behaving as if he were no longer bound by any of the responsibilities of marriage or fatherhood. At the end of what I thought was a counseling session, the priest only told me, "That was a good confession," and nothing more.

Leaving the church, my head was reeling. I had always relied on the Catholic Church for solace and direction. The problems that were overwhelming me hadn't seemed to matter at all to this man. My first thought was that priests are not married, so they don't know what it is like to be in this position. And my position hadn't changed a bit! I was still unsure what to do.

I forced myself to ignore the wild thoughts that had been arising and the outrage at what my husband had done. It wasn't my job to explain my husband's failings. Who would care? His was the kind of behavior that the police would try to explain, or doctors and social workers. The main thing from now on was to make sure that I didn't depend on him in any way or allow my children to depend on him. Never again should I allow myself to be helpless because I was counting on him to do the right thing. I was a survivor!

At that time, I knew that the help I needed would come from God, and I had the strong sense that God had not abandoned me.

The next day, I went to a Baptist church. After visiting with the church pastor, I felt better. I was advised to get a divorce on grounds of the adultery on my husband's part. After this, I started going to this church on a regular basis. That is how I became a Southern Baptist and how God put a beautiful lady friend into my life.

Following the advice I had been given, I sought a divorce right away. The attorney who filed the papers for me seemed to understand my situation. Despite my long years as a devoted member of the Catholic Church, I was not ashamed that I was about to become a divorced woman. I had no choice, and I knew that God supported me in putting the welfare of my children above all else.

In the meantime, I would be responsible for all the bills: house payments, car payments, utilities, and food. Fortunately, I had been saving money over the five years of our marriage and had put aside twelve thousand dollars. One of the first things I had done when my husband began living with another woman was to transfer the money to my older daughter's account. True to form, he did try to clean out our bank account, but there was nothing left.

Now all the costs of supporting our family would be mine to pay. I knew my husband well enough to realize that I would never be able to depend on him again for anything, even for the support money he would be required to pay by law when our divorce was final. I would have to support us by working. But what would I do?

I went to the West Texas University in Canyon, Texas, and inquired about transferring course credit from my university studies in Ecuador. I thought perhaps I could teach Spanish at the community college or somewhere. I was told that they no longer transferred credit from other countries.

My experience in office work was extensive, but my understanding of government and law was only applicable to my own country. My work keeping the accounts for my father's auto parts business had been one of the happiest times of my life. Yet, he was my father, not just a boss, and he appreciated everything I could do to help. Here, there would be too much to learn before I could be an asset to an American company, except perhaps at the lowest level because of my ability to speak Spanish.

Making my cosmetics would bring in some income for my two daughters and me. I called the Food and Drug Administration in Austin, Texas, and inquired about what I needed to start my company in this country.

The person I spoke to did not know; he put me in touch with a man who said that he didn't really know, but he thought a cosmetology license would do it. You see, there is not much cosmetics business in Texas; all the cosmetics industries are on the East and West Coasts of this country. At that time, cosmetology and cosmetics sounded just right to me. I found a cosmetology school in the community college in that area, and on the same day I went to file for a divorce, I enrolled in my new school with determination.

The biggest success in my life so far had been in the cosmetics business. Ironically, if I had let my husband and his mother carry out their scheme to put me to work for them, I would already have known something about the business here in the United States. I didn't waste one minute crying over that missed opportunity!

My skill in compounding chemicals and manufacturing beauty products wasn't going to be any help to me—yet! Here, the courses were geared to people who wanted to learn hairdressing. I had never had any interest until now in this aspect of the beauty business, but, as they say, beggars can't be choosers. I also thought of my children and the possibility that perhaps I could kill two birds with one stone. Anyway, there was nothing to stop me from making cosmetics here. I could work for a living in my own beauty salon and make my cosmetics in my spare time.

It was exactly five months after the birth of my daughter, in 1986, that I began my studies in cosmetology in a Texas school. It would take a year and half to complete all the courses. During the school year, a babysitter took care of my daughter; during the summer months, my oldest daughter, who was in high school, took care of the baby at home, which was a big help for me.

The months ahead from here on were going to be very hard, I knew. I had never thought for a moment that the twelve thousand dollars I had saved would support us for even one year. Yet I also knew that I wouldn't have the chance to support us at all without the ability to earn money, and this was without question the best way to do it, if not the only way.

When my baby daughter was about two years old, her father gave up his rights so that he wouldn't have to pay child support. This was neither a surprise to me nor a big setback. I had been both mother and father for many years, but this was not my first time. Because of my bad choices, life had been hard for me at times but always very rewarding in the end.

There were some really hard times before I finished cosmetology school. I had some wonderful help before the school year was over.

Until then, however, we were doing everything we could to save money. To save on electricity, we were careful to use no more light than we needed, and we let the house become unpleasantly warm from the summer heat. We ate primarily beans, rice, and potatoes, and the taste of meat became a memory. I fed my baby girl by mixing pureed vegetables and beef bones. We no longer took long showers. I could not afford health insurance, so our good health throughout this period was a great blessing, and I thanked God for it every day.

Three months before I got through with school, I was running out of money. The money would not be enough for my house and car payments. I would lose the house and the car that I needed to go to school. All I could do about the situation was pray. What else could I do?

One day, I had an idea. I called the mortgage bank and I asked to speak with a loan officer. I asked him if he could extend my payments until I finished school. He said no, he couldn't do that. But I wasn't going to take no for an answer. I prayed again that night, and I had a better idea. I should speak to the president of the bank; he could make such a decision. So I called again and made an appointment. The president was out of town, but the vice president could see me. I went with my lady friend. We prayed all the way to the bank.

When the vice president came, I told him the truth of my situation: I was not finished with school yet, and the money that I had was not enough to make full payments. Was there any way he could lower my payments for a few months, cut them in half until I started working?

The vice president said, "We've never done anything like this. Please wait, and let me see what we can do." He was gone for about ten minutes, but it seemed like forever. When he got back, he said, "Most people wait until they are delinquent to come for help, but your record of payments is very good, and you are very intelligent to come in before you're in arrears."

My house payments were cut in half for five months, so instead of having the money for payments for five months, I had enough for ten.

The next week, I did the same thing with my car. They allowed me to drive my car for six months without payments, and they extended the payments for six months at the end. The manager of the car company told me that they had never done this for anybody. But then he said, "I don't know why I am doing this, but I am going to help you." He, too, said, "Most people don't ask ahead of time the way you are doing; they wait until it is too late."

Then, I knew that all of this was divine intervention.

I had been taking an English refresher course when I had discovered I was pregnant. I wanted to be able to communicate better with people in the course of my everyday life. English as a second language could be difficult, and each profession required a different vocabulary.

The English I was required to speak and write as a student was harder still. In order to study at cosmetology school, through the teacher, I was able to have two texts: one in English so I could memorize what I would need to know for tests, the other in Spanish so I would be able to understand the material I had to study. It was hard, but not impossible.

# SIX
## Remarriage

Time went by so fast that the years seemed to fly. I was busy from the time I got up in the morning until the time I went to bed at night, raising my child (while my oldest daughter was putting herself through college), running the salon, and making and selling my cosmetics.

My remarriage deserves more than a mere mention because my husband is not trying to control what I say about him or about our marriage, as my second daughter's father would have been sure to do.

I was still going to cosmetology school when a neighbor lady asked if I was seeing somebody. I told her no. "My divorce isn't final yet." She told me that she and her husband felt sorry for me because I was still very young. They knew someone very nice that they wanted me to meet. She described the man, but I was quite sure he would have disappointed me, so I told her I wasn't interested. But my neighbor persisted. "What about Howard?" (This is the name I'm giving a man who lived in the neighborhood.) "He's been single for years." Hearing that, I was sure he had a girlfriend by now.

One day, I saw "Howard" at the post office talking to my older daughter. Since he was much older than my child, I got curious to know who he was, and when we got home, I asked my daughter about this man. She said she knew him because his daughter went to school with her. Other than seeing him around from time to time, I knew nothing about him. But I found out from my daughter that he had been inquiring about me. I asked my daughter if she would introduce me to him. She had nothing to say to me.

A couple of months later, the baby, my older daughter, and I were at the grocery store, and there was Howard. He talked to my daughter while I was standing there, but she didn't introduce me as her mother or anything. This made me angry, and I told her how I felt embarrassed to stand there and be ignored. "Even a dog is acknowledged, and you were making me feel worse than a dog!"

"Mother," she said, "I'm not going to introduce you to him. I don't want you to get hurt again."

This may have been a perfect example of how children sometimes have more sense than their parents.

One day, while I was driving my daughter to work, I saw Howard and another young man working on the driveway of their home. I didn't think anything of it at the moment, but on my way back home, my car stopped in front of his driveway as if by magic. It was some kind of last-minute impulse. I don't remember what excuse I made for stopping, but he came immediately to see what I wanted.

When he got close, I remember thinking that he was a nice-looking fellow. I told him who I was, and he said, "Yes, I know," but after the briefest of introductions, I told him to have a nice day and took off again.

I had amazed myself by what I had done. In my culture, women my age never did anything like that. We waited for men to approach us. But while going to cosmetology school, I had learned that, in this country, women were more aggressive when they wanted something. I may have been forty years old, but I wasn't desperate!

As soon as I got home, I called my daughter and told her that since she didn't want to introduce me to Howard, I had taken care of it myself. She responded by telling me she was ashamed of me. I wasn't hurt by her words. I knew she had been trying to protect me. But I had made the first move, and now it was up to Howard.

A month or so later, one Saturday in the month of June, I had gone to work in my garden after eating a late breakfast. I was wearing an old pair of white shorts. I was young and not bad-looking then. My two daughters, fifteen years old and nine months old, were playing in a small pool in the backyard while I was digging up weeds in my garden.

After a while, my grown daughter told me to watch the baby. "I'm going into the house to get a towel." I continued watching the baby and pulling weeds; suddenly, I heard voices coming from the back porch. I looked up and saw Howard talking with my daughter. When he looked my way, I knew he had come to see me.

I had no makeup on and thought that I must have looked terrible. I wanted to keep digging and bury my head in the sand, but it was too late at that point. *What was my daughter trying to do to me?* I thought. I had no choice but to come and say hello.

This was our first time to see each other after my car had stopped in front of his house a month or so before. We talked for at least an hour. He told me that if I needed anything, he would be glad to help me.

My previous marriage had been such a disaster that it was as if I had been married to the devil himself. This time, I wanted to go with someone completely the opposite. This new fellow was quiet and shy. He didn't smoke or drink and was in every way the opposite of the last man in my life. In some ways, he reminded me of my own father.

I began to ask people about him, because I knew people could look a certain way and not be what they seemed. I wasn't going to make the same mistake as I had before when I had married a complete stranger. Yet most of the people who knew Howard had good things to say about him.

After paying me a few more visits, in September 1986, a month after my divorce was finalized, he asked me out for the first time. I had thought he would never ask.

Since that first date, we were never apart. We dated for eight years before we got married.

In 1994, my mother and father came to visit me from South America, and when they met Howard, they both liked him. Knowing that I had their approval, we made arrangements and got married. My second daughter was nine years old. Things couldn't have been better. But then, six months later, during the first week of December 1994, I had a life-changing experience.

# SEVEN
## Starting My Business

Throughout the school year, I never stopped thinking of how I was going to open my own business. I had a picture in my mind of what it would look like and where it should be located. As for the money needed to open a business like the one I saw in my mind, I had a rough idea of how much I would require, but, as the year wore on, I was no closer to acquiring it. Perhaps I was only dreaming, but I was also praying hard and trying to keep God—the invisible, divine force that is with us always—in my thoughts.

Toward the end of the school year, I began to hear from people who wanted me to work with them or for them. They were people who were in business for themselves. It was hard to resist the pressure to solve my problems by going to work right away, but I stayed firm in my desire to run my own business and be available for my children. My trust in the Lord never wavered during this time.

After a year of turmoil, my divorce became final, and as soon as I got home on that day, I began to cry. I felt so alone. And why wouldn't I? No one in my family knew what was going on. I remember being angry about my life and blaming God. Why hadn't He answered my prayers when I was trying to change my husband's behavior? I swallowed my tears. *Since you didn't answer my prayers, Lord, from now on You will be my husband. You will be the father of and provider for my children.* And that was that.

A couple of weeks before I had to go take my final cosmetology test in Austin, I got a telephone call from my beautiful lady friend, Mrs. Thompson (not her real name), who God had put in my life and who I would later call my "American mother." She told me that she'd seen in the newspaper that someone was advertising a salon for sale. Everything was ready for someone to move in and start working. I told my friend that I didn't have the money, but we could go see it anyway. Before going to see it, we prayed together.

I had Mrs. Thompson beside me and my baby in my arms when we got there. It was a Saturday. The salon was a Morgan building—just what I wanted. When we went inside, I couldn't believe it. This was exactly what I had been picturing in my mind for so long.

The lady who owned the salon said that she had been praying for a buyer to come along who really needed her place of business. My friend spoke up on my behalf and told her, "This lady needs it desperately." I told the lady who owned the building that I did not have the money, but I would take care of some business and get back to her soon. She was willing to wait until she heard from me.

I prayed that night and thought, *What can I do?* Well, I am a businessperson, so I formed the following idea. The next day, I went to the local bank, the same one where I had been transacting all my business for the last five years. I asked to speak with the president. When I went in, I told this man—I'll call him Mr. Mason—that I had come to see him about the Morgan building that was for sale and wanted to know if the bank could lend me the money.

Fortunately, he knew about my misfortune, so he was willing to help. Since I didn't own any property for collateral, Mr. Mason offered to put up the same building as collateral for the loan. I let the president know that I still had to take my test and pass it before I could be bound by the terms of a loan. He understood. The loan would still be available when I got my cosmetology license.

The next day, I went back to the woman who owned the building and told her that I was going to buy it and why I needed to wait for two more weeks. She, too, was understanding.

Two weeks later, I went to Austin for my test. I was supposed to get my license in the mail in about a week to ten days. It took three long weeks to get to me, having been sent somewhere else by mistake. Perhaps there had been a glitch because I was the only student who hadn't taken the summer break and I had finished before everybody else. As soon as I got my license in the mail, I didn't wait to go home; I went straight to the bank to show it to Mr. Mason. We signed the papers, and he showed me out, saying, "Go get your business!"

It took me another couple of weeks to have the building moved to the backyard of my house and get everything ready. On April 7, 1987, I was open for business.

I worked Monday through Saturday, and on Sundays, I did housework. Though I hadn't seen my parents in four years and was homesick, I couldn't afford such a trip while I was establishing my business. It wasn't until 1991, when my parents were having their fiftieth wedding anniversary, that, with much sacrifice, we were able to go. This would be my first break in a long time.

# EIGHT
## New Discoveries

The first time I heard about wanting a specific gender for an unborn child was in the fourth year or so of working in my salon. A new client came in with a child that I thought was a boy. The child was dressed like a boy and behaved like one. Then her mother called the child by name, and I realized it was a girl. While I was taking care of them, the woman said to me, "We wanted a boy, but God sent me a daughter. A daughter who behaves just like a boy!"

*This was exactly what had happened with me*, I thought to myself. I had been hoping for a boy, foolishly imagining that I would be able to change my husband by giving him a son. Hearing what had happened to my client and thinking how the same thing had happened to me, I knew without a doubt that I was the one who had been responsible for creating the tomboy that my second daughter was becoming. And from that day on, I began to pay close attention to female children with boyish ways. Whenever possible, if I knew their mothers or saw them with their mothers when they came to my business, I quietly asked questions about the hopes the parents had entertained when the child in question had been on the way. This was the beginning of the work I began to call my "research."

Sometime thereafter, I was at a Hobby Lobby store and overheard the lady in front of me in line talking to the cashier, who sounded like a friend of hers. The cashier asked the lady about her daughter, and she responded, "Well, we wanted a boy so bad, I guess that's why we got Allison. She's worse than any boy!" They both laughed at that.

I continued working hard. Sometimes, I worked fourteen or sixteen hours a day. God had blessed me with another wonderful babysitter, whom I'll call Mrs. Marshall. She would come to pick my child up, and she would bring her back home. This was a great help to me, and my child loved her. Over time, my business got busier and busier, and I had to work longer hours. I bought a beanbag and placed it in a corner of the salon so that my child could go to sleep there until I got through working. Sometimes, it would be eleven at night before I was finished. On her beanbag, my daughter often drew pictures or looked at books, but she never interfered with my work and was quiet and respectful toward my clients, who loved her. My clients' understanding played a big role in our survival during that time.

When she got to be of an age to start prekindergarten, I enrolled my daughter in the local daycare center. There, she met the first set of twin boys who would fight over her. Their mother kept me posted about what was going on. She was apparently very affectionate toward them.

The whole time, it seemed to me that everyone must have noticed her gender differences. The truth was that nobody did. All the teachers at the daycare center loved her. Some still remember her. She was fluently bilingual from an early age, almost from her first words, and that set her apart from the other kids.

I was her teacher at home in my spare time. She learned to point out many of the countries on the globe. She knew the alphabet in Spanish and could count to one hundred. Her babysitters told me many times that she was a prodigy, a very gifted child. And throughout her childhood, she loved to play baseball in our backyard, to ride her bicycle, and to skate. Really, she enjoyed all outdoor activities.

Things with my family after I remarried couldn't have been better, but six months later, during the first week of December 1994, I had a life-changing experience—one that would affect my physical body in a huge way.

# PART 2
## BODY

# NINE
## My Back Pain

During the holidays, business would pick up and become almost more than I could handle. This year, I wanted to be in the best possible shape for the stressful days ahead. On December 5, 1994, I went to visit a chiropractor. This man gave me an adjustment with what I felt was extreme and unnecessary force. I did not feel good the next day. Two days later, I awoke with what felt like pinched nerves all over my body. The same day, I lost all hearing in both of my ears, my eyes were hurting, and I had a strong pain in the lower part of my head and neck. It was as if I'd been hit with a brick! I continued working despite the excruciating pain.

On January 6, 1995, I was forced to close my business for the first time in eight years. The pain had become unbearable, especially in my eyes and at the back of my head. On January 11, I went to see a neurologist to find out what was wrong with me. After all types of tests, I was diagnosed as having a typical back problem: two bulging, or herniated, disks in my neck. Though the doctor and a second neurologist I visited told me I did not need surgery at that point, the pain continued.

I was very depressed. I was suffering physical pain that I could do nothing about and that was caused by no wrongdoing on my part. In addition to the physical pain and psychological stress I was suffering, I also had to endure very poor treatment from several doctors I had seen. The only doctor who was nice and helpful was my gynecologist, but he could not do anything for my neck problem.

Before long, I had seen a total of eleven doctors. All of them had begun our sessions in a polite and professional manner, but as soon as they found out I blamed a chiropractor for my ailments, their attitudes changed. Most of them treated me as if I were trying to involve them in a medical scam or something. Aside from the repeated embarrassment, I wasn't receiving proper treatment for my medical problem.

I should point out that ever since I was originally diagnosed, I had begun to do research and learn everything I could about my illness. I also tried all the natural remedies I knew of from back home: healing foods, herbs, vitamins, visualization, meditation, positive thinking, exercise, and, of course, prayer. I even went so far as to order a whole pig's neck from my local grocery store. My mother had told me that the pig's biological structure was similar to ours. I wanted to dissect it and see for myself how the neck was put together and how it worked. Not happy with that, I decided to enroll in courses in psychology at Amarillo College, hoping that studies of that kind would help me to figure out what was wrong with me. Throughout this time, I was in terrible pain.

Since I had chosen a business career, I didn't know much about anatomy or biology, yet I was certain that knowledge of these subjects would also enable me to help myself. As part of the general psychology course, along with things that were more directly related to my research, I was able to learn the structure and function of the outer ear, inner ear, and middle ear, as well as of the auditory receptors. I wanted to understand what kind of damage I had suffered when I lost my hearing. I also wanted to learn about my eyes. When I saw the structure and function of the eye, it helped me to better understand where the pain was coming from. Why didn't I just learn anatomy? Because I wanted an understanding of psychology to help me cope with my anger and my psychological stress.

On May 17, 1995, Dr. Andrew Weil appeared as a guest on *Prime Time* to talk about his new book, *Spontaneous Healing*. Along the way, he mentioned ways to heal back pain. He also appeared on *Good Morning America* the next morning. This time, I listened even more intently. He mentioned yet another book on back pain. It seemed too good to be true.

After a painful and depressing Fourth of July, I decided to order the book and others relating to my problem. I read *Spontaneous Healing* first. I was amazed to find out that Dr. Weil had been in Ecuador and other countries to do research, spending a lot of time in the Amazon jungle. Many of the treatments and cures he described were home remedies that I had already tried. He also spoke of how successful his patients' own research had been in the healing process.

A second book was recommended: *Mind Over Back Pain* by Dr. John Sarno. Dr. Sarno is a professor of clinical rehabilitation medicine at the New York University School of Medicine and an attending physician at the Howard A. Rusk Institute of Rehabilitation Medicine at New York University Medical Center. I knew the Lord was guiding me, as I had already purchased this book. The amazing part is that I had purchased it by mistake.

All the books I had been studying—including *The Power of Positive Thinking*, by Norman Vincent Peale, which I had read on my own—were a help to me in reading Dr. Sarno's book. I understood everything he had to say about the mind and body connection. I began to feel better, although I still had some concerns, since I was told by the neurologist not to lift more than ten pounds.

On August 2, after praying that God would show me his glory, I decided to call Dr. Sarno. After a couple of days of trying to connect to his number, I finally got through. His assistant got Dr. Sarno on the phone. I told him that I had read his book but still had some concerns. He was very polite and patient. He answered all my questions and assured me that I would be all right.

By the time I hung up the phone, I felt completely cured. (This was pure mind power.)

I permanently lost 60 percent of my hearing in my right ear, and my eyes still bother me to this day, but I do not have to live with the excruciating back pain.

Meanwhile, my readings in psychology at the college had included Sigmund Freud, Alan Bell, Martin Weinberg, and Sue Hammersmith, among others, on the theory of homosexuality. These were classical, accepted views that I neither accepted nor rejected. I did recognize that they bypassed the opinion I had formed based on the results of my research and my own practical experience with my unborn child.

In my psychology studies, I was unable to find one mind or one voice that spoke to me on this subject from the standpoint of shared knowledge and experience. I knew I had to keep reading, but I would need to consult alternative sources. The kind of knowledge I sought would not prepare me to work within the system. It may have been the knowledge that I was meant to share with others, but it was not the knowledge I wanted to share that would help those with homosexual and gender identity issues understand the origin of their problems, alleviate the guilt they had been made to feel, and help them not to blame the people who had caused their problem out of ignorance.

Already it was clear to me that the way ahead would require me to think "outside the box," as I'd heard it expressed—to "keep my own counsel." I wanted to read more widely. I longed to find medical doctors or educators who had thought through the material they were teaching or who were teaching from their own experience, their own hearts.

When Dr. Weil led me to Dr. Sarno, I knew I had found such a man. I feel I owe it to Dr. Sarno and to others who suffer from back pain to say something about his book. Even though I felt that Dr. Sarno's words to me over the telephone were the main factor in helping me to manage my back pain and evict it from my body, I know that readers of English might have been able to find a solution for their pain from the mere reading of his book.

Early in his book, he explains how most doctors will blame back pain on any deviation from what is strictly normal on an X-ray. Nevertheless, more than 90 percent of structural irregularities in the spine and its associated nerves, muscles, discs, and spurs are not responsible for back pain. He explains that most doctors have a "deeply held conviction that the spine is the source of such pain." For that matter, chiropractors have the same conviction. And as I already knew, having a bulging or "slipped" disc was reason enough for back surgery, which many doctors had already advised me that I was going to need.

Finally, I'd found a man—one man, one doctor—who did not share their opinion. Who, despite the loss of work and income, was willing to say honestly that structural and functional deviations from the norm were no reason for surgical interventions of any kind. For that matter, in Dr. Sarno's opinion, they were no reason for prescription medications. The remedy he suggested in his book was the simplest and most effective ever suggested to me by a medical doctor; he called it "knowledge therapy." He wanted his patients to understand the precise nature of their back problem, as well as the associated pain and loss of function.

According to him, these back problems were caused by circulatory problems—in particular, *ischemia*, or reduced blood supply to certain areas. He identified the cause as tension and called the back condition (often affecting the neck and shoulders also) tension myositis syndrome, or TMS.

A little later in his book, Dr. Sarno writes, "It is difficult to escape the conclusion that conventional diagnoses unwittingly contribute to the severity and persistence of back pain because they frighten and intimidate" (1986, 31). This from a medical doctor! I was weeping tears of joy! At last, the pain that had been causing tears of another kind had been identified for what it was, and the cause of it had been identified as *iatrogenic* (i.e., caused by medical treatment), a big word that was becoming an important part of my English vocabulary!

Ever since the beginning of my back pain, I had wondered why the people of my country never underwent back surgery or suffered from back pain like so many Americans did. Easily half of my clients were complaining of back pain at one time or another. Yet natives of the Andes Mountains, some of them very old, often carried heavy weight on their backs, and none of them were complaining of back pain; nor were they having surgery.

When I was able to heal this pain with the help of Dr. Sarno, whose method consisted almost entirely of applying newfound knowledge and understanding the influence of the mind over the body, I knew that this was the field that I wanted to prepare for: natural healing, or as I would later come to know it, holistic medicine.

From Dr. Sarno, I learned that Americans hadn't always been so dependent on chemical treatment, or "the technology of healing," for their problems. As he says in his book, in what everyone likes to call the "old days" in America, "circumstances required a great deal more dependence upon self-healing, 'nature's remedies' and the like. Patients had not been educated to believe that medical treatment could cure all conditions." A bit further on, Sarno states that "there are untapped sources of healing within us" (1986, 32). Thanks to Dr. Sarno himself—or his voice over the phone—I was soon able to tap into these sources of healing.

But back to the book. Dr. Sarno explains how traction or immobilization of various kinds almost always fails to reduce back pain or prevent its recurrence. And much like Dr. Lipton in my later reading, he disparages the placebo effect. Though almost always effective for a while, pain tends to recur when the placebo effect has been responsible for its alleviation. Calmly, wisely, he explains that when TMS is responsible for back pain, movement is required, not immobilization. As for the placebo effect, "pain is a symptom, not a disease process. It is a signal that something is wrong" (Sarno 1986, 35). Is it so hard to believe that our bodies are trying to communicate with us through our minds, not merely trying to annoy us into paying attention to a particular part of our anatomy?

Anyway, Dr. Sarno has the last word on placebo reactions, and it's common sense, like so many of the things he says: whether placebos are reducing tension temporarily or abolishing pain temporarily, "belief produces the result, suggesting that psychological factors govern placebo reactions" (1986, 35).

On page 41, Dr. Sarno makes the bewildering claim that spinal fusion has lost favor with doctors today. Many friends have told me this simply isn't so. Perhaps it is losing favor with certain enlightened doctors, but many are still doing the procedure all over the country. Not on people like me, however! And anyone who has read Dr. Sarno's book will refuse the procedure (and maybe surgery to correct spinal stenosis as well).

An insurance agent who once worked in bodily injury claims for the nation's largest insurer has told me that never in her experience had she met an orthopedic surgeon—or *orthopod*, as they are sometimes called—who has elected to have a spinal procedure performed on himself or herself. The diagnosis, the prescribed remedies and procedures, and the medical treatment of back problems in general are highly suspect to me now, as they would be to anyone who reads Dr. Sarno's book and accepts his authority.

Sarno doesn't stop at decrying current medical treatments. He calls disc pain a "myth created and perpetuated by the medical profession" (1986, 43). In reading this, I had to keep reminding myself that this man is writing as a medical professional, a specialist in back injuries. In a sense, Dr. Sarno is quarreling with the diagnoses of neurologists and psychiatrists, not just orthopedic specialists. People who might seem jolly often appear to be so because they have learned to put the things that bother them out of their minds.

"This is a foolproof method for generating tension," Dr. Sarno informs us. "Putting things out of one's mind doesn't get rid of them; it simply relegates them to the unconscious" (1986, 53). And, of course, I already understood that the unconscious was in more or less constant communication with the conscious mind. With all the work I was doing, and with one more person to take care of (my husband), I felt as if I had the world on my shoulders!

The precise nature of back pain is examined in detail by Dr. Sarno. There are only three causes of TMS: 1) muscle spasm, 2) accumulated chemical wastes, or 3) nerve pain or irritation (Sarno 1986, 65, 75). I was surprised to learn that all three are a function of poor circulation, and poor circulation is a function of muscle tension. In spite of all the high-tech misbelief, there is nothing more complicated going on.

The confusion isn't entirely the result of doctors being too greedy or too anxious to frighten patients into seeking more extensive treatment. Sarno goes on to say that "tension can produce a variety of physical reactions through the autonomic nervous system, of which TMS is the most common. These reactions appear to be interchangeable, so that one may have heartburn, for example, or symptoms of tension headache instead of TMS" (1986, 66).

Again, doctors are let off the hook by the simple fact that patients "unconsciously . . . prefer not to be considered nervous or jittery" (Sarno 1986, 83). This ties in with earlier remarks about the way stomach ulcers seem to have gone out of fashion. People are reluctant to reveal tensions affecting their muscles, including changes in their breathing and the amount of breath available to say or do something, as this might be seen as a sign of weakness, lack of commitment, or even cowardice. All of us want to appear confident in what we say and do—or sometimes jolly, sometimes blasé, etc. This does not reveal a duplicitous nature; it is merely human.

Dr. Sarno's discussion of the treatment of back pain should be required reading for all who suffer from pain or know someone who does. His "knowledge therapy" took me by surprise. There was nothing I needed to buy. All that was required was that I fully understand what was happening to my body, how my mind was interpreting it, and how to use good sense about the whole process.

Sarno ends his book with words that had enormous, life-changing power for me: "We must learn to recognize nature's truths even though we don't understand them. . . . What we need is a compound prescription of humility, imagination, devotion to the truth, and above all, confidence in the eternal wisdom of nature" (1986, 109).

Partly as a consequence of reading Dr. Sarno's book, I began to take stock of my situation and identify sources of tension. Since pain had made work very difficult for me, after closing my business, I had enrolled in the psychology courses that I've already mentioned (at Amarillo College). Another worry was added as a result: we couldn't manage on what my husband was bringing in from the oil company. (My husband's work for an oil company is too much to go into here. In fact, nearly all the men in this part of the country lived by farming animals, working for the defense industry, or toiling in oil and gas exploration, refineries, transportation, storage, etc.)

When I finally got through to Dr. Sarno, he spoke to me for about ten minutes. He spoke very authoritatively in a beautiful, deep voice. Before I got off the phone with him, my back pain was gone . . . completely.

I think I was healed by the generous, healing spirit of this man, as well as by the words in his book. As I look back, nothing in his book surprised me; I always had the feeling that I was seeing on the pages ideas that already formed in the back of my mind. In any case, he always made perfect sense. And when I heard his voice and felt his listening presence, I had the feeling that we had always known each other. He seemed like a long-lost brother. So, I was changed by his book and recommend it unreservedly to this day, but I was changed by the man as well.

His words were ordinary, yes, but this was not an ordinary man.

# TEN
## Older Brothers

I had some strong hunches about what had happened when I noticed the tomboyish behavior of my second female child, which started at the age of three. Long before I'd read anything about neuropeptides or quantum physics—while the words themselves were still unknown to me—I had begun to suspect that my second daughter's sense of self had been affected by my strong desire to bear a boy with this pregnancy.

I remember having the same feelings with my first child the first time I was pregnant. Her father and I wanted a girl since he already had a boy of his own, and for some reason, I was sure I would have a girl. When my baby daughter was born, I was happy that I got what I wanted. What would have happened if she had been a boy? Now that I know better, I believe I would have had a child with gender identity differences, as my desire to have a girl was very intense.

Nothing from my first experience of becoming a mother had prepared me for the things I had to experience this second time around. In the first place, the pregnancy had taken me completely by surprise. If all went well, I would be forty years old when this child was born. The very possibility of bringing another young life into the world unnerved me.

I was already aware of the ways in which male children received more attention than females in this part of the world. Authority figures were predominantly male. Yes, there were female teachers, especially in the early grades, but children's musical and theatrical activities, so important where I had grown up, were far less important to Texans than the success of male children in playing certain games—especially American football, basketball, and baseball.

The entire town took pride in its best male athletes, and both parents of gifted athletes took special pride in them. In all their activities, even in church, the children who were good at games were given special deference. Team leadership in sports often carried over to leadership in other areas. Gifted athletes were popular with the other children regardless of their parents' standing in the town. And a star athlete conferred prestige on the parents who were raising him, even when there was nothing about their circumstances or attainments that could be called distinguished.

In my husband's desire to be a father, I saw glimmers of the man he might have been. My hopes for our marriage had been dashed not only by his lies but also by his complete loss of enthusiasm for any kind of shared existence. If he were given a son to raise, I was quite sure I would see another side of him, and he would need me as a parent, even if his need for me as a wife continued to be superficial. As time went by, of course, I saw that my hopes for our marriage had been quite foolish and unjustified. The love I had for my children and my intense interest in their activities gradually supplanted any hopes for my marriage. And, of course, I'm principally telling the story of my second daughter; it's a good thing, too. There's very little to say about my ex-husband, and despite the initial shock of confronting a man who cared very little or not at all about his child because of the mere fact that she was female, there's very little of interest to relate about him or "us."

The story I'm determined to tell is about homosexuality: the why of it, the when of it, and how it happens. It must be clear to those of us who are willing to confront the matter openly that our society has fallen short of honesty in this matter, since nearly everybody wants to avoid talking about it.

It's probably not going too far to say that anything having to do with sexuality is treated as if it is dirty and sinful. People with heart, kidney, or lung problems are treated with compassion, but people with sexual issues are excluded, shamed, avoided, persecuted, and, in some parts of the world, even killed. (Consider the important work being done by the near-child Malala Yousafzai to reform the treatment of female children in her native Pakistan.) Girls need help and understanding with their issues just like anyone else. Sexuality in general, even in heterosexual individuals, is a complex world in itself. Everyone is different because the Creator has made us that way.

Over the years, I've noticed that some children are born with the traits of a tomboy (if a girl) or with the effeminate traits of a "nellie" (if a boy) when the parents of such children ardently wished for the child to be born with one gender and the child that was born to them presented with a gender opposite to the one desired. I also realize that each case is different. For example, some children with gender identity differences are very mild cases—enough to be considered tomboys, but they know they are girls and often are attracted only to the opposite sex. Or in the case of a boy, the child might be a little on the effeminate side but go on to live as a contented heterosexual. In others, however, the disorder is stronger. They may be bisexual. In other strong cases, they don't want to acknowledge the gender they were born with. In extreme cases, such people may want to go through surgery to achieve the gender with which they want to be identified.

In my research and observations, I have also noticed that when both of the parents want a specific gender, the combined effort seems to create a stronger energy field. The outcome is, therefore, a stronger case of GID or a transgender child. Though it may seem so cut and dried as to defy belief, it is nevertheless true; according to my observations and careful research over the past twenty-six years, the differences in outcome are due to the energy level that the mother or both parents have put into the thought or desire. For instance, a mild case would be when the mother thinks, *Well, it's going to be another boy, because that's what has happened three or four times before*, and beyond that vague belief, she doesn't put a lot of thought into the matter. A medium case would be when the mother really wants a certain gender and doesn't get it. And, finally, the very strong cases are when the mother and father have an obsession about getting a certain gender, perhaps due to pressure from their families, for example, or because of a previous loss, or for dozens of different reasons that have caused the energy-field level to rise.

Obviously, more research needs to be done on this theory. Unlike a theory that can be proven mathematically, in which the same result is always obtained, it's very hard to quantify actual experience and present convincing statistics. The sample size necessary to do so is almost always very large. Consider the difficulty in presenting the loss of life from the wars in Iraq, for example. On the conservative side, some put the direct loss of life at less than a hundred thousand, while others have convincing documentation that the loss of life is more than a million.

By the same token, people who have religious or political reasons for finding fault with homosexuality are eager to portray homosexual feelings as the entire responsibility of the people who have them, who could change their feelings at will if they were motivated by the right morality—which is always a morality that is in step with the political or religious background of the people who would like to see them changed. Thus, a kind of bullying has been taking place on a huge scale, with those in positions of authority finding fault with people who cannot help themselves and couldn't change their feelings if they tried. This bullying creates hardships for young homosexuals, but it brings hardship for those who bully them as well, since these bullies must bear the brunt of much resentment, especially from members of society who are better educated and more apt to understand the scientific and sociological truths of the situation.

Fortunately, for those of us with eyes to see, predisposed to defuse the hatreds that have been animating the discussion on both sides, there has been an awakening of interest in the issue. About the time that my own interest was awakening in the scientific evidence that was beginning to provide support for my research, *ABC News* came out with a documentary that touched on a lot of important issues regarding homosexuality. Michael I. Silverman of the ABC News Medical Unit reported on this issue in June 2006 with an article entitled "Men with Older Brothers More Likely to be Gay."

Because of its importance, I'm reproducing the entire article below:

> The number of older brothers a man has may influence his sexual orientation, researchers say.
>
> A first-born son has a 3 percent chance of being homosexual, which is standard for the population. However, the fourth son's chance of being homosexual doubles to about 6 percent.
>
> Sexual orientation researcher and study author Anthony Bogaert, at Brock University in Canada, studied 944 heterosexual and homosexual men in Canada, with either biological or non-biological (adopted or step) brothers.
>
> Previous theories suggested that the older brothers' psychosocial interactions with their younger brothers influenced their sexual orientation. If this were true, then the leading factor would be that the younger brother was raised together with older brothers — biological or non-biological.

In Bogaert's study, only the number of biological older brothers, regardless if they were raised together, increased the chances that the younger brother would be homosexual.

"In fact, [the gay men] had more biological older brothers who they were never reared with, which means there's probably some biological prenatal factor to account for this older brother effect," Bogaert said.

His research suggests that, in at least some cases, homosexuality is biological and may account for about one of every 7 gay men in North America.

"This is an important contribution," said Dean Hamer, a researcher at the National Cancer Institute, who discovered genetic links to sexual orientation. "It's possible to really show this is a biological rather than social or psychosocial effect."

This older brother effect "does not explain everyone, but this is definitely a part of it," said Sven Bocklandt, a researcher at the David Geffen School of Medicine at UCLA.

## The Biology of Brothers

The order in which the sons are born to the same mother, called the fraternal birth order, seems to be the source of the biological factor.

"Most studies indicate there is probably a biological basis to men's sexual orientation," Bogaert said. "My study adds to that – it adds another fairly strong piece to the biological puzzle that underlies, at least in part, men's sexual orientation."

The leading biological theory is the maternal immunization hypothesis, which suggests that something changes with each son a mother conceives.

When a mother gives birth to her first son, she may create antibodies in response to the foreign male proteins of her baby. These antibodies can increase in the mother with each successive male baby, which may affect her son's brain, hormones, and sexual orientation.

Some had speculated that there is not a fraternal birth effect; instead, that mothers are simply older when they give birth to their third or fourth sons and that somehow relates to an increased likelihood of being gay.

Bogaert's previous studies found no differences between gay and straight men, regardless of their mother's age when she gave birth to them.

## Lesbians left out

Other factors, such as genetics and prenatal hormones, especially testosterone, probably play important roles in sexual orientation for both genders.

The maternal immunization theory does not apply to gay women.

"The mechanism behind the fraternal birth effect in males is probably gender-specific just to males," said Bogaert. "There are perhaps different biological routes to sexual orientation in women, relative to men."

Bogaert said there is "quite a bit of evidence" suggesting that lesbians tend to have certain characteristics indicating exposure to higher levels of testosterone in the womb, compared to heterosexual women.

Studies have not been able to show an effect of older or younger siblings on female sexual orientation. (Silverman 2006)

This theory seems to have been based on the research and studies done on heterosexual and homosexual men *only*, not based on their mother's experiences. Why haven't we found any answers to homosexuality, gender identity, and dysphoria differences yet? Because we haven't asked the right questions to the right people.

# ELEVEN
## Person-to-Person Interviews through the Years

To demonstrate the truth of my theory, I want to present only a dozen examples from the many cases I have studied. Of course, I have changed their names to protect these people.

- Maria and Lucas have two daughters. The oldest is very feminine, and the second girl has gender identity differences. When I talked to Maria, she told me that since they already had a girl, she and her husband badly wanted a boy this time around.

- Dorothy and Luis have two daughters, and both have gender identity differences. When I asked Dorothy, she told me that she wanted the firstborn to be a boy, but it was a girl. When she got pregnant the second time, she was sure this time that the child would be a boy; instead, she had another girl.

- Mercedes and George have three children; the first and second are boys, and the third is a girl. The first and the third are what we call "normal"; the second has gender identity differences. Mercedes said that since the first was a boy, she had wanted the next to be a girl; instead, they had another boy.

- Sandra and Alex have twins: a girl and a boy. The girl is "normal," but the boy has gender identity differences. When Sandra was pregnant, she wanted twin girls, so one is normal and the other has gender identity differences.

- Rita and Charlie have three daughters, and the second one has gender identity differences. This couple already had a daughter, so they wanted their next child to be a boy; instead, they got another girl.

- Dina and Joseph have twin girls. For Dina's husband, this was his second marriage; he already had a daughter from his previous marriage. She wanted so much for this next baby to be a boy. Their twin daughters are still young, and both are tomboys.

- Rose and Robert have two children; the first is a girl, the second a boy. The first, the girl, has gender identity differences. When I talked to Rose, she told me that she and Robert both wanted the first to be a boy, but it was a girl.

- Virginia and Roy have five children. The first, second, and third are boys; the fourth and the fifth are girls. All are what we call "normal" except for the fourth girl, who is beginning to show signs of unmistakable tomboyish behavior. And why? Because Virginia was sure that she would have another boy. She said that since she had one boy after another, she was sure this would be another boy; instead, she had a girl.

- Silvia, a single mother, has a daughter with gender identity differences. She told me she wanted a boy, but she got a girl.

- Amelia and Jack have two boys; the second has gender identity differences. I asked Amelia if she wanted a girl when she was pregnant with her second son, and her answer was yes.

- Ana and John have six children. The oldest is a girl; the second is a boy; the third is a girl; the fourth and fifth are boys; and the sixth is a girl. All of them are what we know as "normal" except the fifth. This person has a mild case of gender identity differences. You see, the mother had produced a different gender from the previous child four times in a row, so when the fifth child was born, she was prepared for a girl; instead, it was another boy. He is the only one with these traits among his siblings.

- In my own family, my mother had eleven children. All have been thought "normal" except one. My mother lost a child—a boy, my brother—at the age of seven. We all grieved for him, but especially my mother and father. When my mother got pregnant with this particular daughter, both my mother and father wanted this child to be a boy. I do not think that they wanted to replace the child they lost, but a boy at that point would have been a comfort for them. While doing my research, I asked my mother about this sister of mine, who has a strong case of gender identity differences, and her answer was, "Yes, your father and I wanted a boy very badly this time."

In all the cases described above, I saw a pattern, a link between the desire and the outcome. All of these mothers—and, in many cases, the fathers—wanted or wished for a certain gender in their new offspring.

# THE IMPORTANCE OF HAVING AN ULTRASOUND

**Q**: *Ultrasonography is used in pregnancy. Can a sonogram determine the sex of the fetus?*
**A**: It's of great importance that the mother be of one accord in mind, body, and spirit to produce a healthy, well-balanced human being.

Ultrasonography is a noninvasive procedure that has been widely used since the 1970s in hospitals throughout the United States to determine a baby's sex.

As I see it, by informing parents about the sex of the fetus, a sonogram can ease their minds and prepare them physically, emotionally, and even spiritually to welcome the new addition to the family.

**Q**: *Could a sonogram be wrong about the baby's sex?*
**A**: I have spoken to a couple of women who were misled about their baby's gender, but that was many years ago. Ultrasonography has been much improved in the last two decades.

Ultrasound images play an important role when making a decision to maintain or terminate a pregnancy for medical reasons.

Unfortunately, ultrasound imaging is not available in many undeveloped or developing countries. Sadly, knowing a baby's gender is no guarantee that parents will do the right thing. As long as there is such a thing as a "desired gender," babies will be aborted, put up for adoption, or even abandoned.

While she was still very young, I realized that my younger daughter's ways were very different than my other daughter's—ways that were more common in boys, not the sort I was used to seeing in girls. As time went by, I knew I had a tomboy on my hands. Her behavior resembled my GID sister's at that age. For example, as she got older, she liked to watch wrestling matches on TV and other programs that girls customarily don't care for.

Why tell about my daughter? Because I'm trying to be honest about the progression of my emotions, I need to show how my observations were changing how I felt. This progression turned out to be a happy one for both of us, yet I don't want to downplay the pressure I felt at the beginning of my pregnancy and all the guilt and fear that were caused because of it.

From the beginning of my pregnancy news, my ex-husband had wanted our child to be a boy. In the course of my pregnancy, he told me many times, "This baby better be a boy." I did not think anything about it at the time. I knew many women before me had put up with this kind of thing from their husbands. Since I already had a female child, I got excited about having a boy.

In my first pregnancy, I had wanted a girl, and I got a girl. During my second pregnancy, I thought that we would get what we wished to have. I now know that this was ignorance, but because of the pressure from my husband, I felt I had to have a boy. I prayed a lot that my baby would be a boy. We had a boy's name picked out for this baby and many boy baby clothes.

As I have related in "thumbnail" fashion, I had been pregnant for two months without knowing about it. Seven months later, when the baby came, I had a girl's first name ready just in case, but I did not have a middle name. Then, at the first signs of my daughter's tomboyish behavior, I knew in my heart what I had done: my wishing for a boy had something to do with the way my daughter was turning out. Still, this was a feeling I had, not anything that could be proven. It took me many years of research and hard thought before I felt sure of my conclusions.

I finally *know* that thoughts, emotions, and desires in the mother's mind are transmitted by complicated biochemical mechanisms to the fetus's mind, altering the biology of fetal brain cells. The fetus is one with the mother's mental, biological, and spiritual body; therefore, every thought, desire, and emotion that the mother has is imprinted and unconsciously downloaded into the mind of the fetus. The process may sound fantastic and unbelievable, yet the evidence of its truth accumulated with the passing years; finally, medical science rescued me from the suspicion that I was merely "believing what I wanted to believe."

Just as I began to feel more and more certain with the passing years that there was nothing wrong with my daughter being who she was and behaving as she chose to behave, I began to realize that there was nothing wrong with the intuition that had asserted itself the first time I noticed my daughter's tomboyish behavior at age three. At last, I felt blessed by my understanding, and I was grateful that I had done nothing to suppress or encourage it despite the fact that it had made me uncomfortable at times. More than anything, I felt grateful for my second daughter and all that she had taught me with the mere fact of her being.

# TWELVE
## Quest to Vindicate My Intuition

For years, I had been watching my daughter's every move, trying to understand the inner feelings that were directing her behavior. At the same time, I was watching other young children with traits that reminded me of my daughter's.

My daughter was about eleven when her taste for clothes began to be a bit of a problem. A problem for me, not for her! The problem for me was caused primarily by the fact that I was no longer able to influence her choice of what to wear—certainly not as much as I had when she was a younger child.

Shopping with her for clothes or shoes was fraught with frustration for me. When I suggested a certain garment or shoes, she would reject my suggestions, telling me that they looked "too girly" for her.

"But why wouldn't they?" I would reply. "You are a girl!"

"Yes," she would tell me, "but those things are not me."

I already knew what was going on and had come to understand her tastes and expect her choices. I believe I still held the idea in the back of my mind that I could somehow influence her thinking through thoughts of my own. After all, I had caused her perception of herself to come about in the first place by thoughts that I had instilled in her before she was born. By now, I had the strong feeling that I was not the first mother to feel this way.

Thanks to my continuing close observation of children wherever I found them, I had a keen awareness of what was happening right in front of my eyes, and I was completely sure that in my daughter's case, at least, I was responsible for her behavior in some way, if not the entire cause of it. The mental connection between my daughter and myself was still very strong. Why couldn't I undo some of what I'd done by communicating silently and trying to instill an idea of self in her that would more closely resemble the norms of behavior that had been established in this little town?

Yet, my daughter's behavior did not change as time went by. My intense desire that it should was of no use whatsoever, and nor were the words that I was silently communicating. The only change that was taking place was in me! I had begun to feel more and more guilty for my role in my daughter's development. I was praying fervently every day that God would spare her the kinds of harassment and discrimination that had greeted other children during their ascent into adulthood.

Needless to say, I was also mindful of the teachings of the Bible, which had left no doubt in my mind that behavior like my daughter's was not something to be happy or proud about. In addition, I had begun to think that most parents had an agenda for their children—a dream of the future their kids should have. When the reality of their kids' development altered or changed that plan, and destiny took them on a different path, their parents could be disappointed in them— sometimes greatly disappointed.

In discussing my daughter's behavior, I want to point out that the only thing that bothered me and that was different from the girl I wanted her to be was her liking for things that were not considered feminine according to the social standards of the time in this part of Texas. Seen another way, she was more capable than the average girl in a lot of ways, especially in terms of her strength and skill in games. In addition, she was beautiful, confident, outgoing, competitive, and very talented, just as my oldest daughter had been at that age. My oldest daughter is very feminine, just as I am. After putting herself through college and having three jobs at the time, she graduated with a bachelor's in architecture (for which she gave the commencement speech) and a master's in construction science.

* * *

In life, every human being is on a journey of some kind. I told myself many times, *This is my journey, and I will stay with it until I find an answer to my intuition.* We need to understand that there is no one-size-fits-all behavior for humanity. We are all different. God, our Creator, meant for humanity to be like a symphony, in which everyone plays a note and these notes, played together, make beautiful music. Yet some of us seem to have missed the Creator's intention. The stubborn ignorance of such people has made our world a chaotic and hateful place. I understood that as a parent of beautiful children and as a woman who understood her responsibility to others, it was my duty to do all I could to stay in harmony with other people, to love them, and to help them even when they were in some way responsible for painful inner feelings. This teaching was plain to me in the Bible and impossible to ignore.

In some ways, our bodies resemble a mechanical device, but the differences are noteworthy. The body can take care of itself: it heals itself and replenishes what it needs. If it lacks any chemical nutrients, for instance, cravings help to assure that the needed nutrients are supplied. Thus, cravings are a vital feature of the human body. They arise very quickly to assure an adequate supply of food, water, and sex. Even our longing for God is a kind of craving, since the lack of divine connection with the universe is felt acutely by our species even though we don't always understand exactly what's missing or how it should be supplied. Clearly, those who have established such a connection have been rewarded with a more satisfying life; since human beings seem to learn best by example, from the time we are small children, our parents and teachers create opportunities for us to get more out of life by trying to know God.

Yet, without cravings that cause us to feel the lack of a divine connection, we would never make the effort to have one. Thus, our cravings and desires help us to know ourselves and take conscious responsibility for assuring a steady supply of everything we need to survive. All the survival needs of the so-called lower animals are met by instinct. Instinct still functions to supply our basic needs as well, but the need for a divine connection can only be met by consciousness, and the more we acknowledge this craving and strive to satisfy it, the higher our consciousness.

It's easy enough to understand how cravings work in a physical sense to assure our survival. Perhaps it is not so easy to understand how the same type of craving operates in the nonphysical, mind-energy realm of human activity. Various abuses and aberrations have given the word "craving" a bad name in this area, but for the sake of argument, *to crave* has the same meaning as *to want, to need, to desire*. Whenever a human being wants something or has a desire for something, we will find that, as long as the need is real and the mind is accurately projecting that real need, we will be able to understand the meaning of its fulfillment in terms of that human being's survival. By the same token, it is also easy to see when needs arise without a divine connection—for example, needs for pleasure and power. Such needs can be recognized precisely because their fulfillment does not have meaning in terms of species survival. On the contrary, most human activity that takes place without a divine connection has no bearing on our survival and is merely a waste or misuse of mind energy.

Since homosexuality has been a fact of human behavior throughout recorded history, we might well ask ourselves if it has a purpose in terms of species survival. The first thing that comes to mind is "natural population control." Or could the purpose be that it adds diversity to the species? Nature, in its inexhaustible creativity, has given us not one but many, many kinds of each and every species we can think of.

Take apples. There are more than seventy-five hundred varieties of apples (Washington Apple Commission 2010). How many kinds of hummingbirds are there? There are 338 species registered (*Wikipedia* 2015). How many breeds of dogs? According to the Fédération Cynologique Internationale, the largest registry of dog breeds, 339 are recognized. Similarly, cats, elephants, mountains, volcanoes—all things on our planet, organic and inorganic—offer evidence of the complexity of God's creation. Nothing that has been created from the dawn of time was a one-off. There have been no single units, and that includes human beings. Some subspecies, like the Neanderthals, have died out or been assimilated, as we know now from DNA, but diversity is the hallmark of creation and could fairly be said to represent God's plan (or the scientific and mathematical "way of the world," for nonbelievers). Thus, we have different races, colors, heights, shapes, dispositions, beliefs, tastes, talents, etc. The same diversity is apparent in human sexuality.

Does it make any sense to consider that a phenomenon as pervasive as homosexuality is some kind of mistake? Thanks to evolution, everything created achieves greater perfection over time. Could it be that a greater or lesser degree of homosexuality is a kind of natural birth control meant to prevent the species from overpopulating the planet? Love is clearly a basic human need. Without it, life would be meaningless and without purpose. Homosexuals and people with gender identity differences are in no way hindered from expressing such meaningful love; nor is this love any less without the possibility of conception.

If women with gender identity differences are sometimes less maternal and less desirous of bearing children, they are no less willing to adopt them than their heterosexual sisters. Just like men who want to have a family, these women are thus opening doors for children who would not otherwise have a home. And in areas where males are absent (as they are in certain war-ravaged places on our planet), women with gender identity differences have shown themselves capable of doing things that are more difficult for the "girly-girl" to do. Thanks to their more masculine mind-set, some women with gender identity differences are tougher, stronger, and in important ways, less emotional than their more feminine sisters. When extreme life situations require men to take responsibility for child-rearing, they are correspondingly more considerate, sensitive, and gentle.

Can anyone doubt the intention of such a design for the survival of humanity? Again and again, the diversity of human nature assures that the young of our species get what they need to survive, and those who provide it for them do so with satisfaction. To be on the side of survival is to reaffirm the connection to the divine; consciousness of that connection in our lives immeasurably increases the joy we take in being alive.

# THIRTEEN
## My Daughter's Journey

Both of my daughters are talented and artistic, so when my second daughter started middle school, I was very upset to learn that a teacher had misconstrued her drawing of the Chinese yin-yang symbol with what she assumed to be a gang symbol. In fact, yin and yang have been important in Chinese science, philosophy, and medicine for thousands of years. The teacher's action was causing my child a lot of pain and suffering. This was, after all, a child who had been liked or loved by all her previous teachers.

Her problems in this matter had nothing to do with gender identity.

I decided to transfer my daughter to a private Christian school. This was a wonderful transition for her and for me. She had to wear a uniform in her new school, which took care of what to wear. And her new environment was better for her in other ways, more caring and personal. She was now being encouraged to do her art, music, and drawings. She won first place in a state competition with one of her drawings. Her achievements in this area later took her, along with other students from the school, to an international competition in Canada, where she won a third-place prize for her painting. My daughter also loved sports and was a gifted athlete. The school got to compete in volleyball and track, among many other things.

As for me, my studies were proceeding rapidly at this time also. I had already studied the theories of Sigmund Freud as I was finishing my psychology classes in 1995. From that point, I continued to read many informative books, always looking for answers that would provide a connection to my intuition. I was determined to find an explanation for my daughter's behavior and the similar behavior of other children.

Things were normal in my daughter's life for quite a while. I made sure that she had the proper upbringing, and with the many successes she was having at school, she was doing well. The private Christian school was a lot of fun for her. There were some boys that she liked at the school, but I thought she was too young to be dating them. In any case, the school had a policy against dating during the school year. Even so, tension built inside me as my daughter neared adolescence. Anyone could see that she was going to be a beautiful girl, a beautiful young lady. She would be taller than I was, more slender than I had been at her age. In other words, her looks were sure to attract lots of attention; I had secret fears about the kind of attention and who would be lavishing it upon her.

None of these fears ever made it into the open, needless to say. But it wouldn't have surprised me, after reading Dr. Sarno's book, to know that they had made their way into my neck, shoulders, and back.

I was learning to visualize my body and use my mind to control (or at least to try to control) my blood pressure and circulation. Gone were the days when I would confront my daughter about her choices of clothes or playmates or the kinds of activities she enjoyed with them. Instead, I was learning to challenge my own reactions to the issues that were important to me in life and to gain more control over my emotions. Whereas my focus had been on healing after the trauma of my first years in Texas, it was now shifting to prevention.

I was now seeking to control possible negative influences before any damage could be done, and I was succeeding.

As for my second child in school, there were never any problems. I made sure that she would never behave in a manner that would attract negative attention. She was not only a very attractive and intelligent girl but very well liked and one of the top students.

# FOURTEEN
## The Lymphatic System

With the information that I had gathered from Andrew Weil's book *Spontaneous Healing*, Dr. John Sarno's *Mind Over Back Pain*, and also with my recently acquired knowledge of general psychology, I felt that I was equipped to manage almost any scenario involving my health.

Aside from nonmelanoma skin cancer, breast cancer is the most common cancer among women, and the second leading cause of death from cancer among women in the Unites States. It is the leading cause of cancer deaths among Hispanic women. In 2011, the most recent year for which numbers are available, 122,000 women in the Unites States were diagnosed with breast cancer (U.S. Cancer Statistics Working Group).

In 1997, I went to my gynecologist for a routine checkup. I was fifty-two years old at that time. After examining my breasts, the doctor told me that she could feel something in my left breast, and she advised me to have a mammogram. For years, I had been doing monthly self-exams, and I had never felt anything different or unusual in either of my breasts. I told the doctor that I did not believe in having mammograms, did not want to start having them, and was very sure I did not have anything wrong in my breast. Nobody in my entire family has ever had breast cancer. Seeing my reaction, the doctor did not insist.

When I went home, I began my own therapy by changing many things about my daily routine, just in case. The first thing I changed was my diet. And I started to exercise more. I completely stopped using deodorant and began using baking soda instead. And I prayed that God would help me with my state of mind.

That same night, I started to worry. I kept thinking, *What if the doctor is right?* As time went by, I examined my breast constantly, and there were times that I seemed to feel something there. For two years, I worried and worried, but I did not go back to the doctor. I had simply lost confidence in her. At times, my breast was sore. Today, I think it was because I was examining it so often, subjecting it to so much pressure.

One day, after feeling bad all day because I had had a rough night worrying about my breast, I got mad at myself and loudly cried out, "I do not have anything wrong, and I need to quit thinking about this. The doctor does not know my body the way I do."

This happened eighteen years ago. I am still healthy and well.

According to Thomas J. Moore, "It is of extreme importance to have some knowledge of our bodies, and always have a second, and even a third opinion to make sure that the diagnosis is correct. Understanding the lymphatic drainage of the breasts is of practical importance in predicting the *metastasis* (spread) of breast cancer. Interference with the lymphatic drainage by cancer may cause lymphedema (edema, excess fluid in the subcutaneous tissue), which in turn may result in deviation of the nipple and a leathery, thickened appearance of the breast skin" (quoted in Trivieri and Anderson 2002, 60).

After reviewing the epidemic numbers of breast cancer cases in America, I was troubled by the fact that many of these cases are linked to carcinogens, to mammography exposure, or to false positive and negative results; finally, many breast cancer cases are linked to misdiagnosis.

We all know that in these modern times, we humans are exposed to a multitude of dangers that can cause cancer, such as sunlight, nuclear radiation, ionizing radiation, pesticides, herbicide residues, polluted and treated water, tobacco and smoking, hormone therapies, immune-suppressive drugs, food additives, chemicals in cosmetics, mercury toxicity, and chronic stress—to name a few.

Patrick Holford, founder of the Institute for Optimum Nutrition, states, "Most breast cancers are hormonally related, linked to estrogen dominance and progesterone deficiency. Stress, excessive use of stimulants and exposure to pesticides all disrupt hormone balance. Some forms of breast cancer, however, are linked to carcinogens" (1997, 445). Moreover, "hormone therapies that increase the levels of estrogen relative to progesterone in women have been linked to some forms of cancer. In particular, prolonged use of oral contraceptives, or hormone replacement therapy (HRT) for postmenopausal women, have been associated with an increased risk of breast and endometrial cancer" (Trivieri and Anderson 2002, 578).

As I read more and more deeply on the subject, it appeared that my concerns about mammograms were justified.

John W. Gofman, MD, an authority on the health effects of ionizing radiation, spent thirty years studying the effects of low-dose radiation on humans. In his article "Mammograms Add to Cancer Risk—Mammography Exposes the Breast to Damaging Ionizing Radiation," he estimates that 75 percent of breast cancers could be prevented by avoiding or minimizing exposure to the ionizing radiation from mammographies, X-rays, and other medical sources. Other research has shown that since mammography screening was introduced in 1983, the incidence of a form of breast cancer called *ductal carcinoma in situ* (DCIS), which represents 12 percent of all breast cancer cases, has increased by 328 percent, and 200 percent of this increase is due to the use of mammography. In addition to exposing a woman to harmful radiation, the mammography procedure may help spread an existing mass of cancer cells. During a mammogram, considerable pressure must be placed on the woman's breast, as the breast is squeezed between two flat, plastic surfaces. According to some health practitioners, this compression could cause existing cancer cells to metastasize from the breast tissue (quoted in Trivieri and Anderson 2002, 587).

As soon as I read this, I knew that I had made the right decision by refusing to have a mammogram. My stressful experience with my breast took place in 1997 in the state of Texas. My sister then had a very similar experience in 2003 in the state of Florida.

During her two decades as editor-in-chief of the *New England Journal of Medicine*, Dr. Marcia Angell witnessed the escalating corruption in the pharmaceutical industry. Drug companies abandoned their mission to discover and manufacture beneficial drugs and, instead, became "vast marketing machines." As Americans, particularly the elderly, struggled to pay outrageous drug prices, the drug companies gained vast influence over medical research, education, and medical practices. In her expose, *The Truth About the Drug Companies: How They Deceive Us and What to Do About It*, Angell reveals the truth, sympathizes with the deceived American public, and calls for "long-overdue change" (Angell 2004).

Since everything seems to be about money, we need more knowledge and awareness of what is going on around us. We need to solve our health problems with natural cures, healthy nutrition, and a holistic approach that makes use of mind, body, and spirit.

The diet to prevent cancer should consist largely of organically grown vegetables and fresh fruit, whole grains, restricted fat intake, and organic lean meats (avoiding grilled, smoked, and cured meats in particular). For women who already have breast cancer, it is recommended to avoid milk and meat, particularly beef, because of the hormone content. Also, plenty of phytoestrogen-rich foods like beans, lentils, seeds, and nuts should be consumed.

Having all of this information, I now wonder if the doctor who examined me was right or if the holistic techniques I was using to integrate mind, body, and spirit—and the way I was avoiding the mammogram, changing my diet, taking vitamins and minerals, praying, doing visualizations, taking herbal remedies, quitting the use of deodorant, and, most importantly, changing the pattern of my thinking, all in combination—were the reason that whatever I had in my breast went away.

I also sometimes wonder if I had anything at all.

My distrust of conventional medicine was markedly increased by this experience, as it has been by many others I have had over the years.

# FIFTEEN
## Spontaneous Healing

The way my back pain was cured represented a turning point in my life. Until I heard Dr. Weil's ideas on TV and Dr. Sarno's over the telephone and read the books they had written, my experience of medical practice in the United States had been very different from what I had known in my country.

Our hospitals and the doctors who staffed them were very much on the American model, true. Yet patients in Ecuador were more involved in their own care. They represented a long tradition of healing that made use of home remedies that had been passed down for generations. Many of these involved plants that were native to Ecuador, which were used as medicines many years ago in the Amazon basin and became known in the rest of the country for the simple reason that they were effective. Many of the herbs used in cooking were known all over the world, but the herbs used in teas, compresses, and salves were not. Some had no equivalents in English.

In reading Andrew Weil's *Spontaneous Healing*, I was immediately attracted to the idea of a Harvard-trained medical doctor combing the Amazon jungle for medicines being used there by the shamans of a tribe that dwelt in the jungle in which Ecuador and Colombia shared a common border. In the book, he was searching for a certain Pedro, a Kofán Indian. Though Weil was quickly lost in the dense jungle, and the Kofán people he encountered were no help, he managed to enjoy some of the sights. Though his supplies of food were low, when he encountered Pedro's hut—and more shrugs from the Indian woman who was taking care of it—he learned that the famed healer had been gone for ten days. She let young Dr. Weil sleep on her deck in his hammock. After Weil had been bitten and mauled by a jaguar cub that Pedro was keeping in a cage, and after he had waited patiently for a few days, Pedro finally appeared.

Dr. Weil liked him right away but was given no encouragement in his quest because the man who was supposed to have provided him with "insight into the source of healing power, and the interconnectedness of magic and religion" was no longer practicing healing arts (13). Rather, he had become a political activist, organizing his tribe to fight the people from Texaco who were threatening the entire region with exploitation of its oil resources. In a sad postscript to this adventure, we learn that these Indians were virtually wiped out and lost their ancestral lands.

In spite of the failure of his mission in the jungle, which had taken Dr. Weil years of his life and involved many other shamans and disappointments—Pedro had been his last hope—Weil felt that his experience seeking the Kofán marked a turning point in his life. Afterward, he studied healing plants in Ecuador and Peru for a further year and ended his quest for healing medicines.

By then, Dr. Weil realized that he didn't have to search the world over for a source of healing. After four years studying botany, four years of medical school, and nearly as long wandering in the Amazon jungle, he had reached an understanding of what he wanted to do with the rest of his life. He settled near Tucson, Arizona, and stayed there, teaching medicine and practicing a kind of holistic medicine that made use of every known method of healing along with an imaginative mix of naturopathy and conventional medical strategies.

Until I came across Weil's writings, I had been wandering in a jungle of my own. The crowning disappointment for me was when the injury I suffered at the hands of a chiropractor disqualified me for medical care from one physician after another. It was baffling to me that my pain and obvious injury were of no interest to these practitioners. Instead, they were suspicious of my motives in visiting them and contemptuous of the choice I had made to visit a chiropractor in the first place.

I had never considered my daughter's gender differences a problem that warranted medical attention, but I did expect to find—somewhere in the dense forest of writings about homosexuality—that some researchers had explored the possibility of maternal influence as a possible cause for the condition. There was nothing. Yet Dr. Weil was getting my attention by the way he had started his book, questioning the tendency of the medical establishment to treat illness (and just about any unwelcome condition of mind or body) with prescription drugs.

This man had just graduated from Harvard Medical School, yet there was no question of his sincerity and determination. As someone who knew the difficulties of seeking a person, or anything, in the Amazon jungle—relying on the advice of the Indians there to find his way—well, there was no questioning his commitment. He was not some romantic rebel trying to make a name for himself. He knew there were answers to his questions somewhere in the jungle, but since he was the only one asking the questions, there was no ready response for what he wanted to know.

In my own small way, I was doing the same thing. Yes, in a much smaller way, because I harbored no illusions that the kind of research I was doing would be taken seriously. Not yet. But maybe it would be by someone like Andrew Weil.

I understood that I was the wrong person to be asking such questions. If I were a recognized authority of some kind, maybe there would be answers for some of them—or at least the chance of attracting the interest of talented people who would share my concerns and try to help me find some answers. In the meantime, as long as I went about my research quietly, no one paid much attention, and I got the same answer again and again to the one question I was able to ask without upsetting the women who had the answers (who very naturally would have wanted to protect their privacy, especially from a nosy foreigner). And again and again, it was the same answer: yes, while they had been pregnant with the tomboy I had seen or somehow heard about, they had been hoping for a boy, sometimes praying for one. And the women who had given birth to effeminate little boys had wanted a girl very badly, or at least expected one. How could I have been the only person to notice this?

As I read further in Dr. Weil's book, I saw that his years of searching had been motivated by his commitment to healing-oriented medicine. He was collecting small pieces to a very large puzzle. He realized, as I had after coming to the States, that conventional medicine had become "big business." Though individual doctors may have resisted the overall trend, with all the specialties that had sprung up to treat very specific problems, conventional medicine was creating a lot of the problems it was meant to alleviate.

The immediate example that comes to mind, and one often cited by Weil in his book, is the way cancer is treated with chemotherapy and radiation therapy. Of course, the idea behind the treatment is to destroy cancer cells while leaving enough healthy tissue behind for the patient to survive the onslaught. Unfortunately, the way the immune system is compromised by such methods often leaves the patient in worse shape and more vulnerable than ever to life-threatening illness. Many writers have pointed out the way that the complex and expensive sources of chemotherapy and nuclear medicine, in their effect on the immune system, violate the Hippocratic oath to "first, do no harm" (Weil 1995, 36). The technologically complex and hugely expensive mechanisms for cancer care were generating huge profits for the hospitals that installed them and the specialists who understood their operation, but they had little to do with healing.

Weil's ideas were reinforcing a long-held feeling of mine about the way our Western medicine (as opposed to other approaches, like Chinese herbal medicine, acupuncture, and Ayurveda, which I hadn't yet explored) was devoted to curing symptoms, bypassing the body's ability to heal itself in favor of creating a brief sense of wellbeing in the patient. Yes, there can be an improvement after prescription drugs, but wasn't this what was meant by "winning the battle and losing the war"? Traditional medicine's biggest failure was once its biggest success: antibiotics to cure devastating diseases. When he wrote *Spontaneous Healing* twenty years ago, Weil was already aware that the resistance of microbes to antibiotics was increasing, and now, of course, it's of widespread concern to doctors in all the specialties.

Yet Weil was not trying to promote his own ideas at the expense of others. Conventional medicine had its place "on a short-term basis for the management of very severe conditions" (1995, 14). This tendency to incorporate whatever works into his system for health management had great appeal to me. Perhaps he already knew that he was pioneering what would come to be called "integrative medicine."

At the time, I was only aware that I had ventured into holistic medicine and had the strong sense that I was on the right path at last. The health practices of ordinary Ecuadorians in the country where I had grown up had not been stripped of significance by my new country. I had encountered holistic medicine in my readings, but never before had I felt such a personal connection to its philosophy and spirit.

A few years further on, when Weil was established as a professor in the Tucson area (where he would spend the rest of his life) practicing integrative medicine, he found a kind of mentor in a much older man named Bob Fulford, who had often been snubbed by the medical establishment for his way of practicing osteopathy. Some of Fulford's manipulations reminded me of the chiropractors I had consulted in my area on my search for ways of healing my own aches and pains without drugs. Yet despite the differences in the methods they had been taught and in their academic qualifications (though Fulford had much the same education as a DO that Weil had had as an MD), Weil recognized Fulford as the healer for whom he had been searching. When appropriate, he referred his own patients to him, sometimes having to overcome their objections to his methodology, particularly his cranial therapy and vibrating percussion hammer (Weil 1995, 25–39).

This story moved me as an example of the good that can be done by paying attention to all the people we encounter on our path in life who are dedicated to doing good. When their methods are different than ours, we should pay special attention. Weil was a man who was open to all the ways his knowledge and effectiveness as a healer could be increased. This was the path I longed to be on.

Chapter followed chapter with many case histories from Dr. Weil's experience as a practitioner. Therapies included visualization, which was already familiar to me. He also went into his own use of ginkgo biloba to increase circulation, which was also known to me, but it was the way in which drugs of this kind are ignored by the "establishment" that struck home with me. Herbal therapies are considered not "real" because they ignore the accepted biochemical mechanisms—the "magic bullets" that Western medicine prefers for their immediate effect. Naturopathy is scorned for relying on belief systems to profit from its patients, in particular the "placebo response" that cures many people who think they're being treated by a powerful drug and expect immediate results.

I knew from experience with natural remedies in my country and in my own life that results are seldom immediate, as they so often are with potent prescription medications. Still, side effects are fewer, and prolonged use isn't usually fraught with the dangers of resistance on the part of targeted microbes or withdrawal on the part of the patient.

In spite of illusions that have been fostered by advertisers and that have special appeal to the young, we don't live in a world of our own making. Or, if we do, our bodies haven't yet adapted to the futuristic life we want to design for them. We have been designed by God to live in nature, and our bodies are well equipped to heal themselves if we will only reach a better understanding of our true needs and stop making unrealistic demands.

Dr. Weil devotes a whole chapter ("Medical Pessimism") to the way conventional medicine frightens patients about their chances of recovery and increases their despair and the stress levels that are causing many of their problems or at least making them worse. His words about pessimism and stress would have special meaning for me later in my journey; I will go into them more thoroughly when I describe that time.

Weil's ideas about a macrobiotic diet and the functioning of our body's healing system were more familiar. The main surprise for me was in the way a medical doctor had devoted so much time and effort to analyzing all the different ways that people had been getting well for centuries—people like me and, for that matter, all of our ancestors. The case histories were amazing and filled me with hope that I, too, would someday have the chance to heal some of the pain and suffering that people with homosexual issues and gender identity differences are forced to endure because of problems that are totally beyond their control.

No one can understand God's purposes in creating such people, but it is sure that my daughter was one of the healthiest and most well adjusted students in her school, as well as one of the most talented. If I'd ever been worried that she would have a hard time adjusting to life, she had taught me not to worry through the cheerful way she took advantage of what life had to offer, improved herself, and got along with others. Watching her turn out so well had changed me. I was once riddled with guilt for my role in her gender ambivalence, knowing, as

I did almost from the beginning, that I was complicit in it. But instead of merely feeling bad about myself for having been foolish and accepting my punishment, I was beginning to see a way to put my suffering to good account by raising the consciousness of women who had influenced the gender of their children the same way I had.

Throughout his book, Weil refrains from discussing illness as a kind of invasion of wellbeing that needs to be countered with an all-out assault. Instead, he advises us to accept what has gone wrong with us for its ability to teach us about ourselves. Our acceptance will, in turn, create harmony and balance our innate healing systems. With all of the body's resources, including our spiritual resources, engaged in that balance, we can reasonably expect to be healed.

When I read what Weil had to say about the role of the mind in healing, I felt the strongest sense yet that I had been blessed by God to have this book in my hands. Here at last was some of the evidence that I had been searching for—proof that I wasn't alone in my feeling that the mind was capable of influences that conventional medicine could not explain and, therefore, would not accept.

The therapy that excited me so much was called "guided imagery," and the case history was that of his then-wife, Sabine. Sabine was pregnant at the time and had a history of back problems and difficult delivery. The gist of what happened was that her therapist was able to direct her attention to her unborn child and get her to talk to the child and communicate her ideas by intensely focusing on how she wanted her child to respond. By this means, her pain resolved and her pregnancy was spared some dreaded complications.

Later, she went to a hypnotherapist to help deal with problems she anticipated having during delivery. As a consequence, the baby was turned from a posterior to an anterior presentation, her normally long labor lasted a few minutes more than two hours, and the delivery itself was not the ordeal Sabine had been expecting. The entire experience, along with others that were recounted by Weil as he made guided imagery an important healing strategy in his practice, made Weil a self-described "true believer" in the power of the mind to communicate with an unborn child.

Still, I wonder if I could have asked even Andrew Weil at the time to believe in the mind's ability to communicate with a fetus in the first trimester of pregnancy. Clearly, I would have to keep searching for more history of this kind of communication before I would know enough to make my theory believable. If science had any explanation for what was happening, surely I would have read about it by now. So, I was on the right path at last, and I was very happy and grateful to feel that I was headed in the right direction, but the burden of proof was still heavy upon me.

Later in the book are the pages devoted to Dr. Sarno that I have already mentioned. Reading them over, I wondered if I might have been able to solve my back problem with nothing more than the information cited by Weil, had I understood it better at the time. Certainly, I could have if I had been able to draw upon the knowledge of holistic medicine that I have today. At the time, however, the positive aspects of the mind-body connection were harder for me to grasp, especially since I had grown accustomed to the dualistic thinking that prevails in this area, pitting the mind against the body in a kind of battle of wills.

As I see it now, the problems in my understanding stemmed from the fact that I understood the body as the slave of my DNA and was struggling to make my mind its new master. In essence, this was a struggle against nature, since a correct understanding of the natural scheme of things and of the healing system regards the mind as a way of communicating with the body— neither master nor slave, but a means of management and conciliation. Weil is heading in this direction when he advises an end to the battle imagery that prevails in discussing mind-body interactions ("I've got to fight this thing . . .") (1995, 88).

# SIXTEEN
## My Heart Attack

My studies of natural medicine prepared me to face one of the most serious health challenges of my life. Toward the end of March 2011, I was typing a journal as part of my college coursework. At about 3:45 in the afternoon, I suddenly felt a tremendous pressure and pain in my chest unlike any I had ever experienced in that area before.

I had already studied the symptoms and prevention of heart disease, so I knew immediately what that pain and pressure represented. I got up right away and went to take an aspirin. I did not let myself panic; I tried to relax and be calm. Though I felt dizzy and was a little sick to my stomach, I didn't want to call 911. I knew that if I went to the hospital, I would be subjected to all kinds of tests, and in that condition, I would undoubtedly fail the stress tests. That failure could lead to emergency bypass surgery, just as it had for many people my age I'd known or heard about.

I still felt dizzy and weak by evening, so I decided to change my diet. I prayed and made one of the most courageous or stupid decisions of my entire life. I decided to treat my health problem myself using everything I knew. Despite feeling out of breath, I didn't waste time; I began treatment right away.

According to my husband, I was very pale. I didn't let that stand in my way. I made vegetable juice with double the amount of garlic and started drinking an herbal tea. I had acquired my knowledge of herbs from the way I'd grown up as well as from the way I'd been educated. (I'd completed the Master Herbalist program in 2010.) My knowledge and personal experience had made me confident. Since my cabinets were full of organic herbs from my garden, I was keeping a natural remedy for almost anything.

That evening, I made a tea with hawthorn berries and slices of fresh, organic ginger. I also took potassium gluconate along with my regular vitamins A, E, C, D, B6, and B12. Before bedtime, I drank an herb tea of dried, organic, homegrown Saint-John's-wort to calm my nerves. I then tried to rest and relax as much as I could under the circumstances.

Despite the pain I was feeling in my chest, both front and back, I slept enough. Several times that night, I awoke and wondered if I was doing the right thing by not going to the hospital, but my trust in God and in what I had learned gave me the courage I needed to stay firm in my desire to treat myself.

I woke up the next morning with a pain in my upper back like the stabbing of a knife. The pain seemed to be coming from my lungs. When I got up from bed, I felt very dizzy, and I had shortness of breath and a tingling in my left arm. I knew that these were serious symptoms of heart problems. Really, they were symptoms of heart attack, but I still refused to go to the hospital. I knew that with God's help, I could take care of it myself.

So I continued with a rigorous vegetarian diet. I eliminated all fatty foods, such as meat and dairy products, as well as sugar and salt. I was never a big eater of such things anyway, but their complete elimination seemed right at the time. I tried to reduce my stress levels, and I prayed and prayed. Through faith, I knew that prayer would increase my mental and spiritual confidence and that my mental state would be a key factor in my recovery.

Three days later, after the pain in my upper back and lungs had subsided, I felt much, much better. I knew I was not out of the woods yet, but the pressure in my chest and the tingling in my arm were gone for now.

Every night, I continued to drink the tea with hawthorn berries and ginger, and I added some salvia root I had available. I continued taking my vitamins and added $CoQ_{10}$ supplement for heart health. Most importantly, I continued to pray.

Why was I so concerned about surgery, especially heart surgery? I'd heard claims that it could prolong life, but these claims were being debated. When Harvard University School of Public Health put bypass surgery to the test, they concluded that this type of surgery is often unnecessary. There are ways to combat a heart condition with medication, diet, and exercise. Of course, I did not want to take any medication.

Another concern of mine was brain damage; complications like mental impairment and other harmful cerebral outcomes were frequently associated with this type of surgery.

Hawthorn berries may support the heart by increasing oxygen flow to the heart muscle and reducing the inflammation in the blood vessels. It has been suggested that the continued use of hawthorn berries over six months to a year may reverse hypertension. The substance called gingerol in ginger is the main active compound against the effects of heart disease, cancer, arthritis, digestive disorders, and many other major and minor illnesses. Garlic may reduce blood pressure, may lower cholesterol, and may protect blood vessels against blockage. It may act as a natural blood thinner.

There is no heart disease in my family, but I had worked with chemicals for many years, and my bad decisions and wrong choices in life had exposed me to a lot of stress. In addition, all of us are exposed to chemicals in everyday life from processed foods, from pesticides and herbicides, from treated water and toxins in polluted air, from prescription drugs, and from the toxic materials used in dental procedures. In other words, we are being regularly invaded by carcinogenic chemicals.

For an entire month, I had good days and bad, with dizziness and lack of energy, but the pressure and pain in my chest did not come back. When I started feeling better, I continued with my usual exercise routine.

By the middle of April 2011, I had improved in every way, and I felt healthy again. I had lost fifteen pounds, and I was curious to know if my heart had suffered any permanent damage. On May 5, 2011, I went to an alternative medicine center in the city nearest where I lived and had my heart tested.

My heart was not as strong as I wanted it to be, but, for my age, it was all right. I was going to live! I did not take statin drugs or a daily aspirin. As a matter of fact, to this day, I do not take anything except natural, God-made medicine. By controlling my diet and my stress levels, I assure you that I am doing well.

Though I do not recommend that anybody handle heart trouble the way I did, I do think it might be helpful to share a link to the following recent article that came to my attention. The article does not suggest that doctors are always wrong in calculating your heart risk, but it gives reasons that many of them might be; see calculators for heart disease at www.EverydayHealth.com.

# PART 3

## SPIRIT

# SEVENTEEN
## Mind, Body, and Spirit

In 1999, after being in the United States for nineteen years, I decided to participate in the voting process of this country. I wanted to have the benefit of knowing and participating in politics. I had been struggling so hard to survive that, until this point, I hadn't found the time to become an American citizen.

In 1999, I finally applied. After studying hard, I passed the required test, and in August 2000 I became an American citizen. One day, while coming home from the big city, my husband, second daughter, and I saw what we thought was a festival. Since it was still early, we decided to stop and enjoy the music. Just after we arrived—we had just sat down—we heard some noise coming from the people around us, and, all of a sudden, here was Governor George W. Bush coming our way. We stood up and had the chance that day to shake hands with the man who would be elected president that year. My youngest daughter got his autograph. In addition, that year, I got to exercise my new right to vote.

Meanwhile, life was once again giving me the opportunity to kill two birds with one stone—giving me increased knowledge of holistic medicine along with new tools to find answers for my questions regarding gender identity differences.

I thanked my studies in holistic medicine for helping me to understand my second daughter's social development and to profit from what she had to teach me. Still, I never suspected that what I had learned in this area would be limited to my daughter or my relationship to her.

I wrote a paper for college in 2008 based on the incident I'm about to relate, which happened in 2003. The chronology of occurrence seems more relevant to me than the chronology of my writings about life. Ever since I'd begun being interested in holistic medicine, I was having experiences that furthered my interest or made use of my newly acquired knowledge. In 2003, the new person I had become and the new words of wisdom that I held nearest my heart were put to the test.

Before I go on: what words, exactly? The following summation is close enough: We are created as a whole; we come equipped with a system that operates at all levels—mind, body, and spirit. The spirit is the essence of life. The mind is energy that has immeasurable amounts of power. And the body consists of organs, systems, and cells. The mind is divided between the conscious mind and the subconscious mind. The subconscious mind is more powerful than the conscious mind.

Armed with an understanding of how we are connected in mind, body, and spirit, I will speak of my own experience. I felt then—and still feel—that my experiences have been relevant to other people, but I can speak with more authority about situations where all the details and facts are well known to me.

Four years earlier, I had lost a thirty-two-year-old nephew to cancer. At that time, my father, who was eighty-eight years old and very healthy, was witnessing the devastation and terrifying effects of my nephew's struggle with his dread disease. Six months after his diagnosis, my nephew died. One month later, my father became ill. Since I was living in the United States and my parents were in South America,

I was not aware of the situation until my father got very sick and was unable to get out of bed.

When my mother called me and told me of my father's situation, I immediately knew by "intuition" that my father was severely depressed. His doctor was telling him he had cancer. After this diagnosis, he worsened to the point that his body lost all mobility. Without delay, I made a trip back home to see him. With me I took a natural muscle relaxer as well as B complex and multivitamins. (Again, this was before my courses in holistic medicine.) When I arrived home that night and went to his bedroom to see him, his pain was so severe that he was unable to turn his body to kiss me and say hello. For the two weeks before my arrival, he had been virtually paralyzed.

Right away, I told him, "Daddy, you are going to be all right. I brought you the right kind of medication." Then we prayed.

The next morning, while my mother and I were getting breakfast ready, lo and behold, here was my daddy. He had gotten up from bed all by himself and had come to have breakfast with us. (I had not yet given him any of the medications and natural remedies that I'd brought with me.) My mother could hardly believe it. We all thought that his ability to walk again was a miracle. By the third day, my father was dancing (he loved to dance). A week later, we were celebrating his eighty-ninth birthday, and for a further two weeks, he continued to regain his good health.

The second week that I was there, my father had an appointment with his cancer doctor. I insisted that he should not be taken to this doctor because he was doing so well, but my mother insisted that he keep the appointment. Against my will, we all went to the hospital: my father, my mother, a sister who had come to help, and I. When we arrived, some of the nurses could not believe that my father was walking and joking. He was in very good spirits. We sat down in the hospital waiting room, and when he got called in, I went in with him and my mother. After the doctor visited with us, my father was taken to the examining room.

I could hear the doctor asking him, "Do you hurt here?" My daddy's response was no. The doctor continued, "Do you hurt here?" Again his answer was no. The doctor asked the same question several times throughout the examination, and my father's answer was no every time. When they came out to the office where my mother and I were waiting, my father sat down, looking contented and relieved. The doctor came back, sat down at her desk, and told him, "Señor Jaramillo [name changed], you are not hurting now, but you are going to hurt because your bones are deteriorating." When we got out of the hospital, before we got into the car to go back home, my father was sick and in severe pain again.

In the next few days, my father began to fail, and despite my opposition to giving him all the medicine his doctor had prescribed, he took it and got even worse. Two weeks later, he died, not of cancer but of kidney failure.

Why am I telling you this? Because I am going to make a point on the subject of the power and connection of mind, body, and spirit. I will use this illustration to demonstrate how we operate as a whole. We are not composed of separate entities. Every event in our lives affects us mentally, physically, and spiritually. Mind, body, and spirit work together on every level, especially when it comes to our sickness and health.

I will begin by talking about stress, a major cause of illness that affects almost everyone in this modern age. Daily stressors are causing our nervous systems and our immune systems to deteriorate, sometimes taking our general health to extremely low levels.

## How Stress Affects Health

According to Patrick Holford:

> Almost everyone experiences stress on a daily basis. In itself, stress is not a disease. The amount of emotional stress a

person experiences depends on the individual's coping mechanisms. A person's temperament and learned experiences are important psychological mediators of stress and anxiety levels.

Stress can be defined as a reaction to any stimulus or challenge that upsets normal function and disturbs mental or physical health. It can be brought on by internal conditions such as illness, pain, or emotional conflict, or by external circumstances such as a death in the family or financial problems. (1997, 927)

High levels of stress and chronic stress result in a suppression of the immune system, which in turn creates susceptibility to illness, especially to immune-related disorders and cancer. Stress can aggravate numerous conditions, including allergies, arthritis, asthma, atherosclerosis, cancer, colitis, diabetes, emphysema, gastritis, hypertension, hypoglycemia, neuromuscular syndromes, speech problems, and ulcers.

Stress is the consequence of the mind's unrest and, therefore, has a direct effect upon an individual's health. Every action in life requires the use of our minds, as in thinking processes, problem solving, decision making, etc.

**Q**: *What is spiritual health?*
**A**: Now I'd like to talk about how the spirit also influences our health and lives. Fear, anger, lack of forgiveness, resentment, regret, hopelessness, and hatred are some of the emotions that have a negative effect on our spiritual health.

**Q**: *Why did my father's mind and body rest and relax the night I got home?*
**A**: Because of the positive words and our prayer. Faith, hope, and love helped the spirit to rest. That night, my father relaxed and slept better because his mind was not focused on his pain anymore but on new hope and the excitement of my arrival.

Holford states:

> To be spiritually healthy we must consciously cultivate a connection with the spirit, the Divine Life Force that makes all life possible. Self-care approaches such as prayer and the observance of spiritual or religious traditions, meditation, and the practice of gratitude and volunteerism deepen a person's awareness of himself or herself as a spiritual, socially-connected human being. . . . Prayer is the oldest and most popular form of spiritual self-care and has been shown to result in greater feelings of well-being, a reduction in stress, and the rapid triggering of the "relaxation response." (1997, 41–42)

# How the Mind Reacts to Negativity

**Q**: *Why did my father's health deteriorate so quickly after his appointment with the doctor?*
**A**: It was because of negative input from the doctor. Fear took over my father's mind, and his stress level went from ten to a thousand. Conventional medicine tends to be too negative.

In the book *Spontaneous Healing* by Weil, we read:

> Too many doctors are deeply pessimistic about the possibility of people getting better and they communicate their pessimism to patients and families. Many of the patients that come to see me have been told by doctors, in one way or another, that they will not get better, that they will have to learn to live with their problems or expect to die from them, that medicine has nothing else to offer them. (1995, 159)

This lack of hope is what causes many people's health to get worse, and the majority to die, because they are directly affected psychologically, physically, and spiritually.

**Q**: *Why did my father's increase of mental and spiritual stress make him physically ill?*

**A**: Because stress damages immune functions the most. It weakens the body's ability to fight disease and increases susceptibility to infections and illness. The net result of stress in our body is a significant reduction in immune system function.

## Nutrition and Our Health

**Q**: *Why did my father's health get better the first two weeks after my arrival?*

**A**: I took with me B complex and multivitamins. We began by boosting his immune system. How do you boost the immune system? State of mind, exercise, and a healthy diet all play a part in the recuperation process. Calming forms of exercise rather than stressful ones are probably best for immunity. The Chinese art of tai-chi has been shown to improve the count of T cells (one of the body's immune cells) by 40 percent (Holford 1997, 209).

My father loved to dance. We were dancing three days after I got home. We went out shopping and danced again on his birthday. All this exercise was the greatest contributor to his rapid recovery. In addition, the vitamins helped him to regain his appetite, and he began to eat well again. My mother and I made sure that my father received the best nourishment, which you only get at home, nowhere else.

Louis Pasteur, who discovered in the nineteenth century that microorganisms were responsible for infections, realized late in his life that strengthening the body rather than conquering the invading organism might prove a more effective strategy (Holford 1997, 208).

A human being is made up of roughly 63 percent water, 22 percent protein, 13 percent fat, and 2 percent minerals and vitamins. Every single molecule comes from the food that we eat and the water we drink. Eating the highest-quality food in the right quantities helps us achieve our highest potential for health, vitality, and freedom from disease. The immune-boosting nutrients include vitamins A, B1, B2, B6, B12, C, E, and folic acid, as well as iron, zinc, magnesium, and selenium, which are available in a diet rich in organic fruits and vegetables (Holford 1997, 44).

**Q**: *Why was my father in such tremendous pain, to the point of not being able to turn over to kiss me hello?*
**A**: Because when a person is under extreme stress, all the muscles in the body are constricted, and pain is caused by the stimulation of special sensory nerve endings that respond to bodily irritation, pressure, heat, cold, injury, stress, and certain diseases. However, each person perceives pain differently, and that perception can be influenced by any number of factors, including emotional and mental attitudes (Trivieri and Anderson 2002, 662).

## How Drugs Affect the Physical Body

**Q**: *Why did my father's physical body die two weeks after taking so much medication?*
**A**: In *The Peril of Prescription Drugs*, Thomas J. Moore writes, "Injury, even death, from prescription drugs has now become routine" (quoted in Trivieri and Anderson 2002, 46).

Moore is a senior fellow in health policy at the George Washington University Medical Center and author of *Prescription for Disaster: The Hidden Dangers in Your Medicine Cabinet*. He says, "Prescription drugs are responsible for over 100,000 deaths in the United States each year" (quoted in Trivieri and Anderson 2002, 46). Furthermore, Moore points out that one million users are severely injured and another two million are harmed as a result of hospitalization for prescription drug–related problems. So serious is the problem that the use of properly prescribed prescription drugs now ranks as the fourth leading cause of death in the United States. But according to Moore, the extent of the harm is even greater than that due to the lack of figures on the number of patients whose drug-related injuries are sufficient to require consulting a physician but do not require hospitalization. Moore estimates such cases total in the millions as well. These facts justify his conclusions that prescription drugs "rank as one of the greatest man-made dangers in modern society" (Trivieri and Anderson 2002, 46).

Another major problem is the unreasonable expense of prescription drugs. The US Food and Drug Administration's process for approval of a drug costs as much as $250 million and five to ten years of development time. Yet the profits of pharmaceutical companies are among the highest of any industry in the world and often come at the expense of human health. For example, a recent cancer drug, Levamisole, taken in combination with another drug, Fluorouracil, was shown to reduce the recurrence rate of advanced colon cancers by 41 percent when taken following surgery, according to a study conducted at the Mayo Clinic in Rochester, Minnesota. But this same drug, which cost $15 annually when used as a treatment for worms in animals, has a price tag of $1,200 when used to treat cancer patients for the same period (Trivieri and Anderson 2002, 45).

**Q**: *Finally, why did my father die from kidney failure and not from cancer?*
**A**: I believe it was because he was prescribed ten different cancer drugs along with morphine each day.

The detoxification system has two lines of defense. Specific organs prevent toxins from entering the body while others neutralize and excrete the poisonous compounds that get through this initial line of defense. Key components of the detoxification system include the gastrointestinal barrier, including the small and large intestines; the lymphatic system; kidneys, the bladder, and other components of the urinary system; skin, including sweat and sebaceous glands; and the lungs (Trivieri and Anderson 2002, 23).

On television, we continually watch commercials and advertisements for drugs, the majority of which have side effects. One of the serious side effects is kidney damage, among other dangerous and even deadly effects. This painful experience with my father opened my eyes and gave me the desire to explore and learn more about natural approaches to regaining one's health.

# What Is Alternative Medicine?

The words are used simply to denote approaches to health and healing that do not rely on drugs, surgery, or any other conventional medical procedure for treating illness.

As early as 5000 BCE, for example, "physician-sages" who were formulating the healing traditions of both traditional Chinese medicine (TCM) and Ayurvedic medicine (from India) recognized that human beings were composed of mind, body, and spirit. Health represents a harmonious balance among all three of these aspects of existence as well as the free flow of invisible, vital energy (known in China as *qi* and in India as *prana*) throughout the various body systems (Trivieri and Anderson 2002, 5).

In alternative medicine, there are many ways to cope with stress. If stress contributes to illness, then stress reduction should promote healing. This theory for alleviating stress is the basis of numerous relaxation therapies, such as meditation, guided imagery, biofeedback, yoga, and qigong. Other methods for treating stress include dietary changes, herbal medicine, exercise, Ayurvedic medicine, and traditional Chinese medicine.

The treatment of stress is fundamental to alternative medicine. If stress is causing illness, eliminating or reducing it should hasten healing. Meditation is universally recommended for relaxing the mind and body and calming the spirit. Guided imagery helps with specific problems. Yoga helps reduce tension and helps with cardiovascular exercise. Changes in diet should include more sattvic foods (after the Indian model) and the use of traditional Chinese herbs.

According to Larry Trivieri and John W. Anderson, "Health is far more than the absence of disease. When we are healthy, all our bodily systems and functions are harmoniously balanced with our environment. In this state of equilibrium, our defense mechanisms and our immune system can efficiently handle most of the hazards that life presents, whether these are pathogenic (disease-causing) organisms, toxic substances, or stress factors of various kinds" (2002, 9).

According to Dr. Chaitow, positive health depends upon three interconnected factors. The first is the body's structural system, including all of the muscles, bones, ligaments, nerves, blood vessels, and organs and their functions. The second factor is the body's biochemical processes, which involve the absorption and utilization of nutrients, the elimination of waste, and the complicated biochemical relationships that are the key to cellular functions and health. The third factor comprises the mind and emotions as well as the spiritual dimension of each person. "When there is a balanced, energetic interplay among these three components, we have health," Dr. Chaitow says. "But when imbalances exist within any of these factors, or in their relationship with each other, ill health occurs" (quoted in Trivieri and Anderson 2002, 10).

Diet is a major factor in 60 percent of all cancers, so the best way to prevent cancer is to eat only organically grown fruits and vegetables. The organic label ensures that no genetic modifications or carcinogenic pesticides or herbicides have been used in their cultivation. If animal products are consumed, the label ensures that animals raised for food have never been given growth hormones or antibiotics, and pesticides and herbicides have never contaminated their feed. Being richer in nutrients and trace elements than food produced by conventional means, organic foods strengthen the immune system, a factor of great importance in checking the spread of cancer or preventing it outright.

Naturopathy also makes use of herbs and botanicals to prevent and treat cancer. And, of course, drug companies have been hard at work trying to isolate their active ingredients and understand their exact function in slowing the spread of cancer or preventing it in the first place. Some of the herbs that have proven useful include astragalus, chaparral, echinacea, turmeric, feverfew, goldenseal, and wormwood.

Foods with strong antioxidant properties, such as those in the broccoli-cabbage group, have shown specific anticancer activity. The oligomeric proanthocyanidin complexes (OPCs) in grape seed extract are potent antioxidants. Tomatoes help neutralize cancer-causing nitrosamines. The juice of wheatgrass is a powerful tonic and anticancer agent. Many mushrooms fight cancer, especially those in the reishi group and the shiitake, common in Asian cooking. Broccoli sprouts are a rich source of sulforaphane, perhaps the most powerful of anticancer phytochemicals.

In conclusion, stress is the result of our minds going out of control via our thoughts, memories, expectations, regrets, and a lot of "ifs." Our spirit gets involved with the natural reactions of fear, anger, and a sense of despair. (After the loss of a loved one, for instance, many people get angry with God.) We all react in similar ways through difficult times. These negative but human reactions weaken our immune systems and directly affect our physical bodies, allowing them to become ill. Then, as if our bodies didn't have enough to struggle with, we poison them with man-made drugs.

Still, there is hope, much of it coming today from the field of alternative medicine and the holistic approach. I believe that, with time, we will all learn more about our bodies and the natural processes with which we have been equipped, and we will become more aware of the power of mind, body, and spirit. We will also understand how positive and negative thoughts control and influence our health. We must know that we are spiritual beings and that faith and hope are essential for healing. Perhaps then we will also realize that we have been blessed with an amazing, natural, botanical resource that is plentiful, effective, inexpensive, safe, and waiting to be put to use. I also believe that people will begin to take charge of their own health and decision making for a better outcome in the struggle for good health and longevity.

# EIGHTEEN
## The Power of Fields

In 2006, Dr. Wayne Dyer gave a lecture about his new book, *The Power of Intention*, on PBS. Over the years, I had become familiar with Dyer's work as a life coach and tried to keep up with his books. I was always on the lookout for ways to grow as a mother and a person, and Dyer, more than any of the other gurus of the self-help movement, seemed to be disseminating the most useful strategies for self-improvement.

I ordered Dr. Dyer's new book through PBS as a way of making a contribution. In it, Dyer mentioned another book that sounded like it might have particular relevance to the research I had been doing since 1989 with mothers of overt or probable LGBTQ children: *The Field*, by Lynne McTaggart. In this chapter, all page numbers given in parentheses refer to McTaggart's book (McTaggart 2008) unless otherwise identified.

The next day, I went to the bookstore and bought *The Field*. The book was written by an investigative journalist who had conducted a passionate survey of important scientists and their work. These were researchers who had been devoting their lives to understanding how we communicate with the universe and how the universe is communicating with us by means of a zero-point field.

As McTaggart explains, "Zero-point energy was the energy present in the emptiest state of space at the lowest possible level of energy, out of which no more energy could be removed" (20).

When I began to go deeper into this book, I realized that some of the top thinkers in the area of human consciousness—including chemists, physicists, and biologists—were offering evidence that my crude idea of "downloading" information to my unborn daughter wasn't in the least far-fetched. My humble research among the many mothers I'd encountered, which had quietly continued all during my daughter's childhood and adolescence, had placed me on the cutting edge of science. The more I read and understood what these important scientists were discovering in their laboratories, the more I was vindicated in all the questions I had been asking in the laboratory of life and all the nights I had lain awake trying to make sense of my observations and experience.

As the ideas in this book began to flood into my consciousness, it thrilled me that I was able to follow the discussion. My studies had not prepared me to study the actual research, yet the author's enthusiasm for the ideas was contagious. She made me feel that I was looking over the shoulder of these researchers, people who had been willing to follow *their* intuition and risk the scorn or ridicule of well-regarded authorities in order to expand the boundaries of the possible for future students.

From the first researcher under consideration, the astronaut Edgar Mitchell, I knew that this book was going to change my life. Apparently, Mitchell had a personal mission while he was on the moon that went beyond strict NASA guidelines. He had become interested in telepathy and was willing to cooperate with friends back on Earth who had been doing credible research into the phenomenon. Mitchell's qualifications as a scientist with a PhD who had studied astrophysics at MIT and his abilities as a test pilot, which had singled him out for commendation, had set him apart from the other astronauts as the "intellectual" on board. Still, the research into communication that he did on two successive evenings with the little bit of time he had to himself would surely have raised eyebrows among his colleagues on board and back at the space center on Earth, had they known it was going on!

Mitchell's experiments later proved to be successful, but he probably already knew they would be. During his trip (he was the sixth man to walk on the moon), he experienced a kind of spiritual revolution, a peak experience that would forever change his ideas about the way we are connected to each other and to the rest of the universe. The basis for this has often been understood as a connection to God.

With my Roman Catholic education and my acceptance of Southern Baptist theology, I was well schooled in religious belief, but I'd also been trained to believe that there was a separation between the kinds of things that were taught in church, Sunday school, or the Bible and the revelations of science, with its complicated mathematics and endless laboratory testing.

The moment I got my mind around the concept of *nonlocality*, I realized that I was experiencing a divine revelation. In the subatomic world, quantum particles are able to maintain a connection to each other over any distance, so their actions influence each other without any apparent energy source. This was my first inkling that the zero-point field, the main subject of all of McTaggart's research, would reaffirm my lifelong dialogue with God as a source of my intuition.

My prayers had made me receptive. Out of trust in powers that I couldn't possibly understand scientifically or in any language, I would be able to respond in the right way to problems of health and parenting and make business decisions and other life choices without depending on others who may not have had my best interests in mind.

This may seem like a lot to ask of God, but it becomes easier to grasp if we will accept the idea that every human act, from the tiniest movement of a pen to the launching of a space shuttle, has been recorded in some way in the zero-point field. It is as if the gamut of human possibility, as well as of other life on earth, both plant and animal, is being mirrored. The mechanism isn't completely understood, but the proof that the record exists is there if we're willing to look for it.

As I began to read through this book, equally surprising to me was McTaggart's willingness to take on the entire medical establishment with statements like the following: "the entire structure of science, with its highly competitive grant system, coupled with the publishing and peer review system, largely depends upon individuals conforming to the accepted scientific world view" (13).

This is something I had long suspected, but my background had led me to trust that professors and educators were trying to increase my knowledge, and medical doctors were trying to improve my health. I then went on to read how experimentation as sponsored by the agencies mentioned above "is primarily to confirm the existing view of things"—most often, in the development of technology for industry (13).

In reading this book, that was the first of many occasions that I was given an answer to one of the questions that had made me very lonely as I was working away in the dark, asking questions about mothers' feelings when they were pregnant. The theory that had formed in my mind over time, thanks to the way my questions were being answered, would be a threat to well-established systems of behavioral modification.

*The Field* goes on to discuss the work of one of the oldest and most committed researchers in extreme science. Hal Puthoff has long been associated with cutting-edge research applying principles of quantum physics. Puthoff was one of the first scientists to sense the possibility of energy in the zero-point field, but he had been fighting an uphill battle against debunkers. There is much more to be learned from Puthoff than what used to be known as "energy from the vacuum" (19).

The tendency of modern science is to relegate particle research to subatomic situations, but Puthoff saw immense possibilities if only modern physicists would take the zero-point field into consideration. Until Puthoff and others began to look at this field—a sea of energy where particles are always in motion—as a source of energy and power that human beings could use, it had been subtracted out of physics equations: "Because zero-point energy was ever-present . . . it didn't change anything. Because it didn't change anything, it didn't count" (20).

Puthoff and other pioneers were pointing the way for physics to take the zero-point field into account and stop "subtracting out God" (96). By ignoring inconvenient evidence, almost anything can be proved. McTaggart makes the point in her book that the physics of the future will surely embrace the achievements of Isaac Newton, which will no doubt still be important in everyday life, but the way future humanity functions in everyday life will also reflect an understanding of the subatomic world of particles and waves. Much of what is now called "quantum physics" will just be "physics."

While Harold "Hal" Puthoff had been struggling for most of his life to be taken seriously by the academic establishment, he had an angel investor named Bill Church (whose fortune came from Church's Chicken) who knew enough physics to appreciate Puthoff's genius, the difficulty of his quest, and the sincerity with which he was pursuing it. Still, Puthoff would have to work outside the mainstream (if not in the dark) for twenty years before his ideas began to resonate with a young physicist who'd just made earthshaking discoveries of his own, Bernard Haisch. He was later to be joined by Alphonse Rueda and the great Russian physicist Andrei Sakharov (33, 145).

Science fiction writer Arthur C. Clarke immediately grasped the meaning of their work and called it a "landmark" in the history of physics. He acknowledged their achievements in his book *3001: The Final Odyssey* by naming the inertia-canceling drive of his spacecraft

SHARP, from an acronym composed of these researchers' initials (McTaggart 2008, 33).

What happened to the next important figure in the book must be even more disturbing to anyone who understands the difficulties of going against established ways of living and working. Trained in business, I understood the necessity of a status quo. It's hard for people to accept new methodologies when they've been paying the bills by teaching how the system works, making money from the system as bankers and heads of corporations have been doing, or working at highly specialized lower levels in the "technology sector," which has been getting bigger and bigger with the passing years. Still, Fritz-Albert Popp was interested in cancer research.

Vast sums of money have been spent on research into the causes and control of cancer and are still being spent. Popp was one of the brightest stars in German science, and his initial studies were quickly published and much discussed. Popp had discovered that cancer compounds were able to take UV light of a certain wavelength (380 nanometers per second) and scramble it. Cancer researchers had already found (in studies of skin cancer) that the body's own system of photorepair operates on this frequency. No one had ever understood why this should be so, but Popp was up to the challenge. The problem was that no one else in the medical establishment could believe that our bodies were capable of emitting light (39–41).

Much work remained to be done before Popp would be proved right. He had to lose his professorship and for years was considered "radioactive" by science faculties and by students who were being judged by their ability to assimilate the teachings of their mentors (52).

In a strange twist, the man who was most effective in vindicating Popp (Bernhard Ruth) developed a machine to detect photon emissions that is still in use today, some forty years later, *fully expecting his machine to disprove Popp's theories.* However, the results of a strict accounting of photon emissions revealed that our cells do indeed produce light.

Years and years of research in partnership with Popp revealed that cells communicate by means of photon emissions, and the greater the coherence between them, the more effectively they can communicate with each other (42–43).

In this area, many biologists and physicists had done important work that supported Popp. One in particular, Herbert Fröhlich, was most famous for his idea that "some sort of collective vibration was responsible for getting proteins to cooperate with each other and carry out the instructions of DNA and cellular proteins." In his studies, he showed that "once energy reaches a certain threshold, molecules begin to vibrate in unison, until they reach a high state of coherence," at which point "they take on certain qualities of quantum mechanics, including nonlocality. They get to the point where they can operate in tandem" (49).

Popp understood what was happening as a holistic process that depended on one central source. Living beings could interfere with coherence, as cancer does, but they could not originate intracellular communication. All living beings were "sucking" photon emissions, the frequencies of which were as various as the forms of life itself. Popp's fascinating work completely revolutionized advanced thinking about the field and was useful in explaining ancient medical systems that have been getting results for centuries, such as acupuncture, Chinese medicine in general, and homeopathy (53–55).

In homeopathy, for example, "if a rogue frequency in the body could produce certain symptoms, it followed that the high dilution of a substance which would produce the same symptoms would still carry those oscillations. Like a tuning fork in resonance, a suitable homeopathic solution might attract and then absorb the wrong oscillations, allowing the body to return to normal" (54).

Of course, there were no direct correlations between the work of these brilliant physicists and my humble studies of maternal influences on unborn children, but I was learning that all of the natural world is communicating with us and has the ability to direct our body's intracellular communications and to improve the conditions of life for those of us who are willing to follow the evidence and listen to what nature is telling us.

As I read further, I began to formulate what I knew in words that made the most sense to me: *Cosmic emissions may not have meaning to our brains, which are trapped in a fragmentary, self-limited version of reality, but they have meaning to our cells.* Of course, I was no scientist, but in the same way that this book had come into my hands, I was beginning to sense that I would find answers in it to the questions I was already asking. (Say, for example, about the role of proteins in directing intracellular communication.) Some of my questions in this area would be answered by my study of other authors, but for the moment, I could hardly contain my excitement.

For years, I had wanted such a world to exist—a world in which the true nature of existence spoke to us with divine authority, communicating to us as the children we were . . . in which our job was merely to make ourselves available to the meaning of the transmission and show respect for its Creator.

Having opened the door to the mysteries of homeopathy—some of which were already familiar to me—McTaggart proceeded to describe the trials and tribulations of Jacques Benveniste, a research director at the French National Institute for Health and Medical Research, where he specialized in allergies and inflammations and discovered the platelet activating factor (PAF) involved in asthma.

One day, an experiment in basophil granulation went awry when his female research assistant inadvertently caused a sample to be excessively diluted. She was reporting results from a sample that was the next thing to pure water. When the results were repeated, Benveniste, who knew nothing of homeopathy, was put wise by a doctor in his lab who was a homeopath. His experiments were demonstrating one of the core principles of homeopathy, by which "solutions of active substance are diluted to the point where there is virtually none of the original substance left, only its 'memory'" (61).

Over four years with Elisabeth Davenas, the trusted lab assistant who had made the original discovery, Benveniste conducted brilliant experiments using anti-IgE molecules (immunoglobulin E is what causes sensitivity to allergens, and its antibody is a very large molecule that is easy to work with microscopically). As in homeopathy, the greater the dilution of the solution, the greater the effect of specimen anti-IgE on basophil molecules, up to the point of only one anti-IgE molecule left (62–63).

Headlines in the popular press credited Benveniste with discovering the "memory of water." All very good, but many experiments remained to be done in order to understand the precise mechanism by which cells were talking to each other. As with the research done by Popp, it was discovered that oscillation was the mechanism. In this case, oscillation was produced by electromagnetic signals that could be amplified and digitized in the manner of sound waves (61, 70).

Benveniste's experiments were widely copied, but they were very sensitive to method and even to the electromagnetic signals produced by a certain female lab worker. Predictably, Benveniste had to submit to what he called "fraud squads" of quackbusters and debunkers. As with earlier articles in *Nature* that had put a disclaimer on his findings, now the prestigious *Lancet* was doing the same thing. After thorough experimentation to prove him wrong, it was conceded that Benveniste was proving something with his experiments, though no one could say exactly how. He wasn't a philosopher of science or a theorist, and he wasn't a physicist. He had strayed into the area of advanced electromagnetism. Though he couldn't explain the memory of water or the ability of molecules to vibrate at extremely high or low frequencies, he went doggedly ahead with his laboratory proofs of these phenomena (64–73).

How well I understood the feeling of amassing data that no one appeared to care about. But if the world was failing to pick up on the work of France's most likely candidate for a Nobel prize—and failing only because the science that would explain what was going on in his experiments didn't exist yet—what chance did a small business owner in West Texas have of attracting attention to a means of communication for which there was, as yet, no mathematical or scientific basis?

Karl Pribram was doing research into rats' brains. The gist of what he was trying to prove sounded incredible on the surface: that rats, and even humans, could still carry out learned behavior without their brains. Later, Pribram teamed up with Nobelist Dennis Gabor, who had discovered holography (78–82). Pribram's experiments had to do with how the eye was processing visual signals. The focus of his work was on how the brain processed interference patterns: "Any optical image could be converted into the mathematical equivalent of interference patterns, the image that results when waves superimpose upon each other" (82–83).

Holography carries the process a step further. Classically, a laser beam is divided so that one part focuses on an object (a teacup, for example) while the other focuses on an arrangement of mirrors. These beams are then brought together on photographic film. The photographic plate records squiggles and concentric circles, but a detailed image of the teacup floating in space is achieved when a light beam from the same kind of laser is passed through the film (83).

This kind of information helps us to understand how our brains are able to reconstitute the image of, say, an apple, exactly where we think it is. We are living in a virtual world, then, but our way of situating the objects in it is incredibly sophisticated!

A team of neurophysiologists at UC Berkeley, Russell and Karen DeValois, were able to convert simple plaid and checkerboard patterns into Fourier waves and then learned that cats' and monkeys' eyes were responding to interference patterns rather than to the images themselves. Building on this work, Pribram was able to see that the brain sorts through frequencies by means of a kind of filtering envelope that prevents us from being bombarded with data from the Field (86–87).

Further studies by Pribram showed that the brain was able to communicate with the rest of the body and control motion by a series of waves and patterns instead of images. Along the way, he uncovered evidence that the senses of smell, taste, and hearing also responded to frequencies (87). Pribram concluded that this decoding was taking place not in a particular site in the brain, but in the spaces between neurons, where chemical charges build up in synapses. Tiny filaments called dendrites penetrate this intercellular space and carry decoded information to other brain cells (88).

Many years later, a certain Walter Schempp, a mathematics professor at the University of Siegen in Germany, finally proved Pribram's theories of the way the brain was decoding information while he was inventing the MRI machine. Pribram's theories were also confirmed by the work of Peter Marcer, a British physicist who needed a machine like Schempp's to prove his own mathematical theories. Schempp and Marcer corresponded with Pribram, and all three eventually decided to work together (88–91).

In time, Stuart Hameroff, an anesthesiologist from the University of Arizona, and Kunio Yasue, a physicist from Kyoto, Japan, contributed research, and a groundbreaking conclusion was reached. In a process called "superradiance," macrotubules create a global coherence of waves, enabling photons to travel along light pipes as if they were transparent ("self-induced transparency"), penetrating macrotubules throughout the brain, and processing information from photons all over the body. The process may well account for our unity of consciousness—the fact that we don't think of many different things at once (91–93).

According to McTaggart, "Consciousness was a global phenomenon that occurred everywhere in the body, and not simply in our brains. Consciousness, at its most basic, was coherent light" (94).

Nature was "making use of a cohesive learning feedback process of information being fed back and forth between organisms and their environment. Its unifying mechanism was . . . information which had been encoded and transmitted everywhere at once" (95). The brain is "a receiving mechanism" that "retrieves old information the same way it processes 'new' information—through holographic transformation of wave interference patterns" (95). Memories can't be burned away, because reception mechanisms can be found all over the brain, and memories are retrieved when cells are in tune with the field: "This kind of interaction might account for intuition or creativity—and how ideas come to us in bursts of insight. . . . An intuitive leap might simply be a sudden coalescence of coherence in The Field" (95).

In concluding this chapter, the most exciting piece of scientific writing I had ever read, McTaggart says, "Modern physicists had set mankind back for many decades. In ignoring the effect of the zero-point field, they'd eliminated the possibility of interconnectedness and obscured a scientific explanation for many kinds of miracles. What they'd been doing, in renormalizing their equations, was subtracting out God" (96).

Similar experiments by Charles Tart at Berkeley proved that receivers hooked up to machines to measure heart rate, blood volume, and other physiological changes were sensitive to painful shocks he was administering to himself, but not on a conscious level. It would have been possible to say to him, "I feel your pain, but I'm not aware of it" (127).

To test our ability to communicate our feelings or desires to animals, Braud designed experiments using the knife fish and Mongolian gerbils. Both species were able to respond to a human desire that the fish change their swimming direction or that the gerbils run faster on a treadmill. Braud was even able to keep red blood cells from bursting when a fatal amount of salt had been added to their Petri dish—by mere wishing (129).

Finally ready to start experimenting with people, Braud began with classic studies of staring. Subjects would stare at a figure on a monitor, and the figure, in another room, would note if and when he or she felt stared at (though they were advised not to think about it during the period of the study). All of these studies were successful, convincing Braud that people responded to remote attention, and if the subjects were introduced to each other and became used to looking into each other's eyes prior to beginning the test, they consciously wanted the staring to continue when they were separated. In other words, we crave attention from people who have already noticed us (130–31).

Studies with Marilyn Schlitz, an anthropologist who had worked with Helmut Schmidt, proved that the researchers could calm down high-strung people using something akin to the staring technique of earlier experiments. The success of all these experiments displayed a progression from the fish studies to the people who wanted to know each other, with the greatest deviation from chance displayed by those who really needed the influence that was being applied (to calm them down, for example) (132).

According to McTaggart, "quantum mechanics govern living systems, [and] quantum uncertainty and probability are features of all our bodily processes"; when "two people have a 'synchronized' bandwidth, the observer with the greater degree of coherence, or order, influences the probabilistic processes of the less organized recipient" (137). Thus do the more ordered affect some quantum state in the less ordered and induce more order.

Moreover, "the model suggested by Braud's work, is of a universe, to some degree, under our control. Our wishes and intentions create our reality. . . . Be careful what you wish for, thought Braud. Each of us has the ability to make it come true" (138).

It is further suggested by Braud's studies that "our dreams, as well as our waking hours, may be shared between ourselves and everyone who has ever lived. We carry on an incessant dialogue with The Field, enriching as well as taking from it. . . . What we call 'genius' may simply be a greater ability to access the zero-point field . . . In that sense, our intelligence, creativity and imagination are not locked in our brains but exist as an interaction with The Field" (139).

After years of such experiments, Targ and Puthoff had reached the same conclusion. Quite simply, the zero-point field was a "giant cryptogram, continually encoded with every atom in the universe, [which] held all the information of the world—every sight and sound and smell" (159).

Reading of these experiences was simultaneously exhilarating and sad for me. It was exhilarating to realize how much work was going on that would take humanity to new levels of meaning and, if enough people could be reached with the information, new levels of under-standing. Yet the powerful of the world were those who controlled the wealth, and business as usual was preserving that wealth. Huge leaps in consciousness were being recorded and then put quietly away, out of the reach of ordinary people and many not-so-ordinary people, until such time as the old ideas that had been enriching the powerful were no longer profitable.

The zero-point field was not only bombarding us with quanta in all kinds of ways; it was giving us the chance to communicate with a higher reality, the highest truth about the universe. We had enough intelligence to begin doing so, as well as the patience and the cour-age to face the findings and be honest about what we found, but be-cause this research was in its earliest stages, most of the people willing to conduct it lacked the money to continue their studies even when the results of those studies were successful. In fact, none of them could be disproven—only challenged and sometimes ridiculed by the onslaughts of debunkers and media naysayers, who were always well funded by the powers that be. Commercial prosperity was preventing the work that was most important to humanity as a whole—since it sometimes involved our very survival—and the best our leaders could do to soften the blow was to hide the evidence or imply that "further study" would take many long years and that it would be foolish to ask for anything now.

In related speculations, William Braud considered the possibility of changing the course of a disease: ". . . it wouldn't be that you could undo [a disease that had developed]. But some of the most harmful aspects of it might not have been actualized yet and might still be susceptible to change. You'd catch a disease at a point where it could be swayed in many directions, from good health to death" (quoted in McTaggart 2008, 175). McTaggart sums up Braud's work by asserting the following astounding possibility: "It might well be that every moment of our lives influences every other moment, forward and backward" (175).

I didn't immediately think of all the situations I would be able to change or repair. The point was to be able to change the course of disease by "one neuron being fired and not another" (as Karl Pribram proposed). Instead of obstinately following paths that tradition or old advice had laid out for us, we could train ourselves to be more receptive to quantum processes. It seemed to me that the only obstacle was the need to know what to pray for and how to be more open to the right influences. In any case, our lives can only be enriched by an awareness of the possibilities available to us; I thank McTaggart for giving us the chance to consider them.

McTaggart's book concludes with a section on the ways we are tapping into the field, first and foremost in the area of healing. Elisabeth Targ, daughter of Russell Targ, teamed up with a psychologist and researcher named Fred Sicher. The two prepared complex, airtight experiments in the tradition of Elisabeth's father. In addition, they began to study the field of healing to recognize leading figures for use in future experiments. They were encouraged by much of the work that had been done by a pioneer in the subject named Dr. Bernard Grad of McGill University in Montreal, for example, who had proven that seeds treated by a healer grew taller than the control batch and that conversely, in a later experiment, negative feelings could influence the growth of plants. Growth of seeds was suppressed when using water that had been held by a depressed man and normal in the control experiment. In later experiments analyzing water by infrared spectroscopy, Grad "discovered that the water treated by the healer had minor shifts in its molecular structure and decreased hydrogen bonding between the molecules, similar to what happens when water is exposed to magnets." Grad's findings were confirmed by other scientists (183–85).

Targ and Sicher examined many studies because many studies had been done of all aspects of healing. Ultimately, their own study was carried out with forty carefully selected healers: "The results were inescapable. No matter which type of healing they used, no matter what their view of a higher being, the healers were dramatically contributing to the physical and psychological well-being of their patients" (190–92).

Many studies have since confirmed the work of Targ and Sicher, and many more are going on all the time. Certain general conclusions can be made. Illness can be healed through a collective healing spirit: "Information in the Field helps to keep the living healthy. It might even be that that health and illness of individuals is, in a sense, collective" (194).

It can also be concluded from these experiments that fear and solitude are the greatest obstacles to healing. Even more astoundingly, individual consciousness doesn't die.

Meanwhile, startling results were confirming the existence of a collective consciousness. Dean Radin and Roger Nelson, both doctorates of psychology at Princeton who had cooperated in PEAR studies, were on the trail of some collective phenomena that could be traced by refinements of a random event generator (REG) machine— FieldREG and PalmREG (201–06).

Radin's interest was first quickened by the way a REG machine responded to the verdict in the O. J. Simpson trial: "The television audience was stunned by the jury's decision, and so were five other silent observers—all REG computers, one at the PEAR lab, another at the University of Amsterdam and three more at the University of Nevada. . . . Like everyone else in the world, these computers had snapped to attention to find out whether O. J. was innocent or guilty" (200).

When he teamed up with Nelson, who had done similar studies with REG machines, many experiments were carried out to prove the reaction of REG machines to all kinds of events. Highly emotional meetings, Broadway shows, even Wagnerian operas were sampled to record increases in the intensity of the spirit or "vibe" that was taking place. The conclusions were inescapable: the REG machines had been "a kind of thermometer, measuring the dynamics and coherence of the group . . . intense moments of like-mindedness seemed to gather enough power to impart some order on the chaotic purposelessness of a REG machine" (205).

The ultimate effect of such experiments was to hold out hope to humanity: "Good might be able to conquer evil after all. We could create a better community. We had the collective capacity to make the world a better place" (212).

In her final chapter, McTaggart assesses the work of all the scientists surveyed and the net effect of their contributions to science. Against tremendous odds and often at the expense of a more comfortable life for themselves, these men and women had relentlessly sought answers to questions that various research establishments in our industries and schools have just as relentlessly refused to ask. They weren't inspired by a desire to prove others wrong, win glory for their brilliance, or, at the very least, receive recognition of the validity of their efforts after long years of working in the dark. These were revolutionaries who were changing the basis and meaning of all scientific research.

If we had reached the end of the atomic age, as Hal Puthoff suggests, and stood at the door of a zero-point age, we might as a species learn to recognize that "people are indivisible from their environment. Living consciousness is not an isolated entity. It increases order in the rest of the world. The consciousness of human beings has incredible powers, to heal ourselves, to heal our world—in a sense, to make it as we wish it to be" (225). Above all, there would no longer be two truths, the truth of science and the truth of religion: "There could be one unified vision of the world" (226).

Because there had been only one reality all along.

I was awed by all that I had read. My understanding of the world had been changed forever. There was no group to join, no reason to take sides with a cause. Instead, I was inspired to read more and to ask more questions. I felt more grateful than ever for the faith that had seen me through thus far and more capable than ever to make a difference—not only in the small world I inhabited but in other worlds I didn't even know about yet, in which there might be a use for my vision and the understanding I had gained and would continue to gain.

Above all, it was inspiring to know that the world was full of caring people and that someone like Lynne McTaggart, not a scientist herself, had spent years finding out what scientists had to say. I was also inspired because, thanks to the clarity of her writing and the sincerity of what she was trying to say, even someone like me, reading about them in a second language, was able to grasp what they had to say.

I would never be a scientist any more than I would be a professional painter after making that critical decision all those years ago. But if I stayed firm in my quest to understand the science that was involved in what had happened to my daughter and learned everything I could about the possible mechanisms involved, I might come up with things that would someday get a scientist's attention.

After reading *The Field*, I was ready to believe that anything was possible—with coherence, with clarity of mind, and with purity of purpose. And in trying to find that coherence, I was not alone.

# NINETEEN
## The Power of Belief

Wayne Dyer was also responsible for the next reading experience that would change my life. Early in 2007, I was watching Dr. Dyer promote his book *Excuses Begone!*, and he mentioned a book by a certain Bruce Lipton that sounded like it might be something I needed to read. The book, *The Biology of Belief*, has gone on to become a best seller, and Lipton has become a kind of guru for people trying to expand their consciousness along certain lines. Page numbers given in parentheses without other information refer to this book (Lipton 2005).

To be honest, as I began to read it, I wondered if his book was what I was looking for or what I needed to find.

In an engaging way, Lipton describes the chaos of his life. He had been going through a terrible divorce, didn't like his new living quarters (where he was robbed in his first week of occupancy), and was fed up with his career teaching histology and cell biology at the University of Wisconsin Medical School. After a kind of breakdown, he took a job on the Caribbean island of Montserrat teaching medical students who wanted to improve their grades and attend front-rank medical schools in the United States.

His first test of more than a hundred of these students was based on tests he had administered back in Wisconsin. The students failed miserably. But in a life-changing moment, Lipton the teacher rose to the occasion and promised to do everything in his power to help these students learn everything that they needed to know to pass such a test, even if he had to teach additional classes at night. The students responded by showing new enthusiasm. They began asking the right questions and helping each other, the better students helping the weaker. In the end, they were able to pass the same final exam Lipton had been giving to his students back in Wisconsin.

Right away, I recognized the operation of "coherence" as I had learned about it reading *The Field* (as well as love and compassion as I understood them from many sources).

I saw that Dr. Lipton was a great teacher and someone who could switch gears when he had to and pour huge reserves of energy into new ideas . . . because he was also a maverick. What had made teaching cell biology so hard for him in the first place was his conviction that Lamarck had been right about the influence of environment on evolution and Darwin had been wrong to put so much emphasis on the gene (creating a doctrine of genetic determinism that was to become even more of a founding principle after the discovery of DNA).

The astounding theory that came to Lipton down in Montserrat had to do with the fact that cells were directing their own growth and behavior by means of input from the environment . . . and that the work of cells, which he had been studying all his life, could be controlled by beliefs. He makes it plain in his introduction that his book will show his personal transformation from atheist to believer, from a Newtonian world view to one more in keeping with new discoveries in quantum physics, and from someone who accepted the dominance of Darwin and genetic theory to someone who recognized the role of environment in shaping who we are and how we think about who we are.

I was captivated by the man's ideas, but until I understood that he was used to teaching rooms full of students and using imagery that would resonate well with them, I was still a little cautious about what I was getting into. The way he describes protein molecules and their ability to change shape is easy to understand. By means of photo illustrations, he shows amino acids as plastic beads strung out on a child's necklace, the basic units of construction of our cells' more than one hundred thousand proteins. Besides their order by color on the "string," the effect of their activity is further modified by placement. He illustrates the existence of a "backbone" by joining PVC conduit in various configurations. The final conformation of the proteins' "backbone" is affected by positive and negative charges. (There's more about electric stimuli later on.)

Next, he shows how the cell's membrane operates using integral membrane proteins (IMPs), both receptors and effectors.

To illustrate the work of the cell membrane, which is the heart and soul of Lipton's theories—believe it or not, philosophical speculations and spiritual knowledge as well as extreme science—he has to delve further into the workings of the cell at the most minute level. To make the process plain to his students, Lipton has designed a bread-and-butter sandwich with what appears to be an inch-thick layer of butter interpenetrated with olives that have been stuffed with pimentos, as well as other olives with no stuffing that have merely been pitted.

This homely image recurs throughout the book. When Lipton stopped using it, his students apparently complained. In time I, too, appreciated its usefulness in describing extremely complicated biological processes. Further on, he uses idea imagery that might resonate even better with today's audience: "The first big-deal insight . . . is that cells and computers are *programmable*. The second corollary insight is that the programmer lies *outside* the computer/cell. Biological behavior and gene activity are dynamically linked to information from the environment, which is downloaded into the cell" (92). Then, further on the same page, "Data is entered into the cell/computer via the membrane's receptors, which represent the cell's 'keyboard.' Receptors trigger the membrane's effector proteins, which act as the cell/computer's Central Processing Unit (CPU). The 'CPU' effector proteins convert environmental information into the behavioral language of biology" (92).

This comparison has an interesting history. Trying to define the character of the cell membrane for his own satisfaction, Lipton came up with "the membrane is a *liquid crystal.*" Later, in the wee hours when he was having these thoughts, he came up with "the membrane is a *semiconductor.*" Still later, trying to work in a description of a most important class of effector proteins called channels, which let in cell nutrients and let out waste matter, he ended his description with "the membrane contains *gates and channels.*" His final description of the cell reduced to "the membrane is a liquid crystal semiconductor with gates and channels." As it happens, he had just bought a nontechnical guide about how computers work from Radio Shack. In the introduction, he found a definition of a computer chip as follows: "A chip is a crystal semiconductor with gates and channels" (90–91).

Despite the preoccupation of most biologists with genetic determinism, "leading edge cell research, which continues to unfold the mystery of the Magical Membrane in ever more complex detail, tells a far different story" (92).

Lipton moves from the nuts and bolts to the holistic world with the surprising revelation that there are hundreds of thousands of IMPs embedded in the cell membrane, doing a multitude of tasks that support systems as diverse as our own: digestion, respiration, elimination of wastes, etc. Special proteins protect DNA with a kind of "sleeve" and do "read-outs" of genetic information, but Lipton declares the membrane to be the brain of the cell. In an amusing twist, he sees the cell's DNA as its "gonad." "Confusing the gonad with the brain is an understandable error because science always has been and still is a patriarchal endeavor" (66).

By the midway point in this exciting book, it becomes clear that traditional teaching about the body has been wrong in many respects, and, given the truth about the mechanisms, many anomalies and unusual findings can be readily explained. There are twenty-five thousand genes, not one-hundred-twenty thousand, as originally thought: "Multicellular organisms can survive with far fewer genes than scientists once thought because the same gene products (protein) are used for a variety of functions. This is similar to using the twenty-six letters of the alphabet to construct every word in our language" (106). Cells can survive quite nicely without a nucleus for a couple of months . . . They only die because they can't reproduce. The membrane, with its attendant IMPs, supplies all of the cell's needs.

Perhaps because of the way Newtonian linearity has dominated thinking about our bodies, causing us to concentrate too much on human accomplishments in engineering and construction, the real story of evolution might be quite different than we had imagined. For example, the evolutionary advantages of eukaryotes (multicellular organisms) over prokaryotes (unicellular organisms, including bacteria, which ruled supreme on earth for billions of years) have to do with the surface area of their membranes.

Bacteria can get along nicely without a nucleus and still display a kind of primitive intelligence (in finding a food source or avoiding a toxin, for example), but their membranes are limited in what they can take in, usually by a very specialized environment. With multicellular organisms, the membrane continued its work of selection and refusal by entering the cell and surrounding organelles, as well as by expanding in size until it was many thousands of times bigger than a bacterial membrane.

The history of what Lipton calls "the language of energy" is also fascinating, especially now, while many of the givens of modern knowledge are being revised. The explanation of the role of constructive interference and destructive interference harks back to *The Field* and the theoretical means of communication wherein interference patterns create a record of our physical behavior and energy emissions, including our thoughts. He even gives us a brief history of electrotherapy and the invention of chiropractic, which along with other drugless practices like homeopathic healing and radioesthesia were taking business away from the medical profession.

He reserves particularly sharp words for drug manufacturers: "I believe the major reason why energy research has been all but ignored comes down to dollars and cents. The trillion-dollar pharmaceutical industry puts its research money into the search for magic bullets in the form of chemicals because pills mean money. If energy healing could be made into tablet form, drug manufacturers would get interested quickly" (112).

All through his book, Lipton points the finger at prescription drugs as completely useless in altering biological processes. For the most part, they merely provide fast-acting, instantaneous relief of some symptom at the expense of creating systemic imbalances all over the body. The example of antihistamines that make us drowsy is given, but there is hardly a drug on the market these days that doesn't have side effects.

From Lipton's remarks and others by scientists who are willing to honestly assess their profession, I was becoming even firmer in my decision never to touch prescription drugs, even if I were advised that my life was in the balance. He decries drug-pushing physicians as "patsies" who get their advice from drug reps, who are nothing more than the "errand boys of the corporate healthcare industry . . . We have been programmed by pharmaceutical corporations to become a nation of prescription drug-popping junkies with tragic results" (109).

Summarizing what we have learned up to the section about mind over body in chapter 15, "Spontaneous Healing," which was of special interest to me for obvious reasons, Lipton prepares us for some of his most important revelations, including the one that gave him a title for his book: "We learned that . . . the functions of cells are derived from the movements of their protein gears. The movement generated by assemblies of proteins provides the physiologic functions that enable life. While proteins are the basic physical building blocks, complementary environmental signals are required to animate their movement. The interface between environmental signals and behavior-producing cytoplasmic proteins is the cell's membrane. The membrane receives stimuli and then engages the appropriate, life-sustaining cellular responses. The cell membrane operates as the cell's 'brain.' Integral membrane receptor-effector proteins (IMPs) are the fundamental physical subunits of the cellular brain's 'intelligence' mechanism. By functional definition, these protein complexes are 'perception switches' that link reception of environmental stimuli to response-generating protein pathways" (128).

With this understanding, we've reached a place where we can consider the relationship between our brains and the cells responsible for coordinating "the dialogue of signal molecules with the community" (131). In higher life forms, specialized cells took over the regulation of signal molecules, providing a nerve network and a centralized processor, the brain: "The brain controls the behavior of the body's cells. This is a very important point to consider as we blame the cells of our organs and tissues for the health issues we experience in our lives" (131).

In a subchapter dealing with the way we feel the language of cells through our emotions, Lipton mentions Candace Pert's *Molecules of Emotion*, which was the next book I would buy in my quest to understand the language of the cell. I already had a strong intuition that this knowledge was going to have great significance for my personal quest.

Lipton's assessment of Pert's contribution is worth quoting at least in part. He notes that Pert's "study of information-processing receptors on nerve-cell membranes led her to observe that the same 'neural' receptors were present on most, if not all, of the body's cells. Her elegant experiments established that the 'mind' was not focused in the head, but was distributed via signal molecules to the whole body. As importantly, her work emphasized that emotions were not only derived through a feedback of the body's environmental information. Through self-consciousness, the mind can use the brain to *generate* 'molecules of emotion' and override the system" (132).

Concluding this subsection, Lipton observes that "our responses to environmental stimuli are indeed controlled by perceptions, but not all of our learned perceptions are accurate . . . Therefore, we would be more accurate to refer to these controlling perceptions as beliefs" (135). *Beliefs control biology!*

Ruminations about belief lead Lipton to a discussion of placebos and nocebos. His quote from Henry Ford says it all: "If you believe you can . . . Or believe you can't . . . You're right!" (quoted in Lipton 2005, 143).

In the discussion of stress, Lipton covers a lot of familiar ground: "Almost every major illness that people acquire is linked to chronic stress. . . . chronic stress is debilitating. A community can easily survive short-term stress like an air-raid drill, but when the stress goes on and on it results in cessation of growth and the breakdown of the community" (152–53). Research into the causes of depression has targeted stress, which has been "overtaking the monoamine hypothesis in recent years . . . (and positing) that depression is caused when the brain's stress machinery goes into overdrive. The most prominent player in this theory is the hypothalamic-pituitary-adrenal (HPA) axis" (Holden 2003, 810–13).

I have long been interested in stress as a cause of cancer, perhaps the most important cause, but the next chapter and final chapter ("Conscious Parenting") vindicated my intuitive sense that Lipton was going to help me arrive at a deeper understanding of what had happened with my daughter.

Lipton cites a work by Thomas Verny and John Kelly. Verny was "a pioneer in the field of prenatal and perinatal psychiatry" (which immediately went on my list of books to buy). While acknowledging the "overwhelming influence" parents have on their children's mental and physical development, Verny is quoted from his landmark book *The Secret Life of the Unborn Child* saying that parental influence starts before the children are born: "The influence of parents extends even to the womb . . . The fetal and infant nervous system has vast sensory and learning capabilities and a kind of memory that neuroscientists call 'implicit memory'" (1981, 156).

In his *Life in the Womb: The Origin of Health and Disease*, Dr. Peter W. Nathanielsz asserts that "a wide range of . . . chronic disorders, including osteoporosis, mood disorders and psychoses, have been intimately linked to pre- and perinatal developmental influences" (quoted in Lipton 2005, 157).

Nathanielsz describes "programming mechanisms" that Lipton prefers to describe as epigenetic mechanisms. Lipton calls Nathanielsz "brave" for citing Lamarck in his book: "the transgenerational passage of characteristics by nongenetic means does occur. Lamarck was right, although transgenerational transmission of acquired characteristics occurs by mechanisms that were unknown in his day" (157).

In his lectures, Lipton likes to show a video from an Italian program about conscious parenting that shows the parents of an unborn child having a loud argument in the course of a sonogram: "You can vividly see the fetus jump when the argument starts. The startled fetus arches its body and jumps up, as if it were on a trampoline when the argument is punctuated with the shattering of glass" (176).

Again, Verny writes, "Awake or asleep, the studies show, they [unborn children] are constantly tuned in to their mother's every action, thought and feeling . . ." (1981, 173).

And Lipton weighs in: "What the father does profoundly affects the mother, which in turn affects the developing child. For example, if the father leaves and the mother starts questioning her own ability to survive, his leaving profoundly changes the interaction between the mother and the unborn baby . . ." (173).

My own situation could have been the one under discussion.

In the addendum to his book, Lipton finally acknowledges that the "environment" of which he speaks throughout the book is . . . the universe. He then begins a philosophical discussion based on everything he has learned since his peak awareness in Montserrat at the beginning of the book. The addendum is as revealing about the man Bruce Lipton is as his introduction was, and his personality and the tensions of his life have made his personality an important ingredient in getting his message across. His book clearly communicates the excitement of his discoveries and his relentless quest to get to the bottom of biological processes that are just now beginning to be understood.

Yet along the way to proving his work, Lipton never loses an opportunity to bring his students along on the quest. He is ever a teacher, and he teaches with his life and puts himself at the center of his experiments. He does so again in a second addendum, in which he introduces psychotherapist Rob Williams, whom he met at a conference all the way back in 1990 when they were both presenters. Since that time, both have lectured in partnership and Lipton has adapted PSYCH-K (a system of muscle testing invented by Williams) to his own presentations.

Earlier in the book, Lipton showed us how muscle testing works. Usually, the deltoid muscle is tested. The person in search of the truth about something extends his arm straight from the shoulder, and the tester presses down on it gently. If the seeker's answer is correct, the arm will resist and can only be forced down. If the seeker is mistaken, the arm will give way reflexively.

A short time after my readings of Lipton and Pert, I was guided to the work of a man who has built an entire system of thought around muscle testing, and he turned out to be one of the most inspiring teachers I would ever encounter on my journey. In keeping with my system of introducing the important people of my life as they came into it, I will only mention his name at this juncture: David Hawkins, MD.

It's easy to understand the spiritual significance of muscle testing. How could there be a more direct way of establishing the fact that the truth about ourselves and about our lives—about everything—comes not from our minds and our thoughts about ourselves but from a complete record of everything, which is available at any time of night or day from the zero-point field?

Though Lipton's book came along in 2005 and *The Field* appeared in 2003, I had hoped to see more sharing of ideas or at least of terminology. Still, it was gratifying to read kind words about the work Candace Pert was doing, which is still attracting scientific attention long after her tragic death of cardiac arrest in September 2013.

Lipton's willingness to work with others and incorporate their thought has been exemplary. Lipton has also shown himself willing to forsake the laboratory and the classroom to try to get his message across to the masses of common people, in which I include myself, who get facts about their own biological systems from drug companies and from the medical establishment, both of whom feed greedily off of their ignorance. In addition, these establishments try to maintain that ignorance and, in many cases, our rather profitable bad health by forcing us to live in a fog of misinformation.

From my reading, it was driven home to me again and again that correct thinking about health problems, gender problems, problems of depression or substance abuse, other behavioral disorders, and spiritual problems would not be found along the traditional pathways of medicine or science, which had been contaminated to some extent by the profit motive.

It would have gone against my cultural background, as well as my training, to be suspicious of people who were trying to make an honest living by teaching or healing with knowledge they had legitimately obtained. Yet I had become very suspicious of teachers or healers who seemed to want me not to think, not to ask questions, not to question what I was told, and not to consider my personal experiences and my all-important sense of self.

Right at the end of his book, Lipton has important things to say about how our bodies are personalized on a molecular level by self-receptors called human leukocytic antigens (HLA). The seemingly miraculous idea that came to him years ago in the Caribbean and sent him screaming to the library in the middle of the night to share it with drowsy students should be just as miraculous to us. We are receptive to signals from the environment or universe because "every functional protein in our bodies is made as a complementary 'image' of an environmental signal. If a protein did not have a complementary signal to couple with, it would not function. This means, as I concluded in that 'aha!' moment, that every protein in our bodies is a physical/electromagnetic complement to something in our environment. Because we are machines made out of protein, by definition we are made in the image of the environment, that environment being the universe, or to many, God" (188).

Of course, I was one of the many who believed in God, but I had already come to believe that the best way to know God was to decode his messages from the zero-point field, some of which had personal relevance to me and completely explained the ability of God to be everywhere at once and have personal meaning to billions of people. Lipton makes an important point when he compares us to television sets in yet another homely image. When we are forced to switch from one set to another, "The death of the television set as the receiver in no way killed the identity broadcast that comes from the environment . . . Because of our preoccupation with the material Newtonian world we might at first assume that the cell's protein receptors *are* the 'self.' That would be the equivalent of believing that the TV's antenna is the source of the broadcast" (190–91).

An important point, since *my* biggest "aha!" moment in reading Candace Pert would come from her claim that "the body IS the unconscious mind." (This formulation is given interchangeably with ". . . the subconscious mind.") Its integrity as a receiver is unquestionable, but its primary use is for quick consultation by the conscious mind, a quick reading of reality that is more accurate than what one can gain from the senses, saturated as they are with images, desires, and the deceptions of others.

And, of course, I should have seen this truth about the subconscious as soon as I understood what Lipton had said earlier when indirectly quoting Pert about the way the same neural receptors were present on most, if not all, of the body's cells. Where God is concerned, we are and always have been available on a physical level. So there is nothing abstract or sentimental about the Indian greeting with hands clasped together in front of oneself—the "*namaste*" that supposedly means "I worship the God in you." Messages of extraordinary complexity are being delivered every second of our lives, endlessly given to us and capable of being influenced by us, especially by our beliefs. Our bodies are vast libraries of spiritual information, frequently in the form of biological information that is being transmitted chemically or neurologically.

Even our so-called common sense, the kind that might most easily be related to things we were told as children or the deep messages of our parents' desires for us, could be understood as a message from the field if only we would bother to test the truth of it and disentangle it from the chaos of our personal experiences and the self-serving images of ourselves that have resulted from those experiences.

# TWENTY
## My Brother's Struggles with Cancer

In 2012, in partial fulfillment of course requirements, I wrote about what happened when my brother was diagnosed with stomach cancer back in 2008, the year I began my studies in holistic medicine. In 2009, I earned my holistic health practitioner license. Unfortunately, I couldn't help him then as much as I could have later, when my studies were more advanced. Still, I was able to help him enough.

I called my paper "Cancer: Stress Misdiagnosed and Mishandled?" I now feel that the title summarized the main points I had been trying to make.

First, I summarized the findings of the World Health Organization's media centre in 2012:

> . . . We have these staggering figures of cancer deaths around the world. Cancer is the leading cause of death worldwide and accounted for 7.6 million deaths (around 13 percent of all deaths) in 2008. The main cancers are as follows: Lung (1.37 million deaths); Stomach (736,000 deaths);

Liver (695,000 deaths); Colorectal (608,000 deaths); Breast (458,000 deaths); Cervical cancer (275,000 deaths).

About 70 percent of all cancer deaths occurred in low-income countries. Deaths from cancer, worldwide, are projected to continue to rise to over 13.1 million in 2030.

In my essay, I am going to talk about cancer and stress. I have lost several of my family members, many of my business's clients, and several friends to cancer. I have seen the cancer process unfold, and noted the stressors that I believe to be the main cause of this illness.

On January 5, 2008, one of my sisters in South America called to let me know that our younger brother was deathly sick and had been diagnosed with stomach cancer. My brother and my sister are two years apart, and they have always been as close as twins.

Right away, there was a problem: I was not supposed to know about his cancer. My brother made my sister promise that she would not tell anyone about his illness. During the phone conversation, my sister also said that our brother could not afford to pay for the cancer treatments. About four years earlier, we had lost a nephew to stomach cancer, and, a month later, our father was diagnosed with prostate cancer. I was not present when my nephew died, but in an earlier essay, I have already described my father's struggle with the disease—or with its diagnosis!

All of this took place before I began my education in holistic medicine. Even so, I already saw that my father's illness had been the byproduct of a strong case of depression and sadness because of the death of his young grandson, my nephew. This experience with my father had taught me a lesson about cancer and stress. Consequently, when my brother could not afford to pay for the cancer treatments, his predicament gave me hope. Immediately, my husband and I made a trip to Ecuador. I took with me vitamin B total, multivitamins for men, my Bible, and some college papers for a general psychology course I had taken in 1995. Call it intuition, but I had an idea of what I was going to do about my brother's cancer.

When we arrived at my parents' home, my mother came to meet us. Sadly, my brother did not want to see me. I understood his motives.

The next day, my sister had to trick my brother so that he would come home with her. When I opened the door, *I could not believe what I was seeing.* My brother was skin and bones, and when he kissed me hello, he was burning up with fever.

Immediately, I asked him to sit down and said: "What is wrong with you?"

He started to cry and murmured: "I want to die."

We all convinced him that he was going to be all right. That night, we prayed with him and for him. He took the vitamins, but he could not keep anything in his stomach. In addition, my brother could not stay still. He was a nervous wreck. Before he went back to his home, I told him that I would expect him to come every day to eat the meals with us that we would be cooking. The second day, my brother came for lunch, but he could not eat because his stomach would not allow him to retain any food. We prayed again. I massaged his tense shoulders that felt like rocks because of muscle tension due to his stress.

The same day, when my brother came for supper, he felt a little better. He was able to eat a little bit and have a couple of swallows of herb tea to calm his nerves. We continued praying and giving him the vitamins, herb tea, love, and positive reassurance.

The third day, my brother's fever was completely gone. We had not given him any medication, not even an aspirin. He continued taking the vitamins (vitamins will improve the appetite). He continued to eat better and drink the herb tea. We were cooking organic, nutritious foods. We gave him a lot of fresh fruit juices, fresh vegetables, beef liver, all kind of grains, etc. In spite of his condition, my brother was still working. I guessed that it would have been more stressful for him not to work.

The fourth day, he was more relaxed, and he ate much better and drank his herb tea. On the fifth day, when he came in, he was smiling. It was wonderful to see him in good spirits. He even asked if my husband could go to work with him. On the sixth day, he was eating like a horse, drinking his herb tea and feeling better. That same night, the sixth, I told my sister, "We have given our brother spiritual treatment through our prayers, love, and positive reassurance. The body has been treated through vitamins, food nutrients, and herb tea. The only thing left to do is to treat his mind. I need to talk to him to find out what is bothering him."

My sister replied, "He won't tell you anything. He is an introvert."

"We will see," I said.

When my brother came the seventh day, I told him that we needed to talk. We went into a room, the two of us, and I said, "I need to ask you some questions." I could clearly see I was making him uncomfortable. He relaxed a little when I showed him the papers from college that proved I had taken psychology. Then I asked him about the divorce he had gone through a year earlier. When I mentioned his divorce, he started talking.

He was full of hatred towards his ex-wife. He had been hurt tremendously by this woman, who is an attorney. She had made sure that my brother wouldn't get anything. That was why he couldn't afford the cancer treatments. Anger about his situation had been consuming him for the past year. To make matters worse, his ex-wife would not let him see the children. When I asked him, "Have you tried to talk to your children?" his answer was no.

"Okay. You must call them today and tell them that I am here and I want to see them."

The children were fifteen and thirteen years old at the time. They came the next day. I talked to them also, and, the next weekend, my brother and his two children went on a hiking trip. In two weeks, my brother gained ten pounds. He was himself again, and I made him promise not to go to a conventional doctor anymore.

Through the illness ordeal, I never mentioned the word cancer to my brother or that I knew anything about his cancer. I only told him that he was depressed and anemic. Three weeks later, when we were coming back home, he was so grateful. With tears in his eyes, he told us that he would take care of himself in the future.

All this happened seven years ago. He is still alive and doing well.

According to *Chronic Emotional Fatigue: Why It Affects Your Mind and Body . . . How You Can Stop It!* by Billie J. Sahley:

Stress is a subjective and personal effect. What is stressful to you may not be to someone else. People react differently to various situations. Just because something does not cause stress to others does not mean it might not be stressful to you. Stress triggers can come from a variety of sources including overwork, addiction in either yourself or a loved one, death of a loved one, divorce, lack of sleep, changes or loss of employment, increased use of tranquilizers, antidepressants, or pain medications, unexpected illness or anything that taxes you mentally or physically. Both positive and negative stressors are taxing, even if a change is for the good. It may involve readjustments, uncertainty and anxiety. Other sources of stress might be negative thinking habits, a high-strung or impulsive character, emotional drains, social pressures, conflicts, confusion, frustration, loneliness and boredom. Even certain diseases, injuries, pain, chemical or radiation exposure, and drugs can be the catalyst for stress. The warning signal for danger comes when small stresses begin to combine, multiplying their effects, especially when they remain unresolved . . .

Over the past ten years we have done extensive research at the Pain & Stress Center on the physical and mental effects of stress. Stress causes a slow deterioration of your immune system and your mental functioning. One day, you just cannot seem to get it all together, and you are overwhelmed by fear and confusion which add to the effects of stress.

## Physical Symptoms:

Headaches, neck and back pain, aches all over, muscle spasms, high blood pressure, crying, digestive problems, strange heartbeats, facial tics, never feeling well, constant anxiety and depression, inability to concentrate, use of antidepressants, pain medications, tranquilizers, or daily alcohol ingestion. These signs are evidence that stress is having a serious effect on your body and mind. (1995, 25–26)

People who, like my brother, have been diagnosed with cancer or any incurable disease become submerged in a deep depression. Some of these people have a sense of worthlessness and a great amount of fear, shame, and anger. They become isolated. They may feel guilty about things over which they have no control. This behavior is typical of people who have been given devastating news about cancer or any incurable disease. The shocking bad news changes their personality and behavior.

According to *Quantum Healing: Exploring the Frontiers of Mind/Body Medicine* by Deepak Chopra, MD:

> With stress, we noted that as part of the overall reaction, the stomach and intestines stop digesting food. As long as the stress reaction is temporary, this is completely normal and a correct thing for the body to do and it happens automatically . . .
>
> However, if you choose to stay in an environment where there is constant stress, the time must come when your body wants to return to digesting food. Then a deep conflict will arise, because the stress reaction will still be saying 'no' to the stomach while another part of the brain (probably the hypothalamus) is saying 'yes.' The resulting turmoil ties the stomach in knots and churns up the intestines. These organs begin to lose their natural rhythm, and if you do not give them a chance to return to it, they will become victims of wrong memory, just as surely as an addict does. The stomach will start pouring out gastric juice at the wrong times, the colon will go into spasms and the smooth linkage between the whole gastrointestinal system will collapse; hence the burning ulcers, and chronic irritated colon experienced by many people under high stress. (1989, 84–85)

I have always heard that one has fever only when there is an infection somewhere in the body, but a person under extreme stress can also come up with fever. According to Online Medicine Tips, stress causes fever:

> One of the factors which [has been] found to cause fever is stress. During stress, the body tends to be on overdrive. This causes certain abdominal functions to occur in the body. In order to cope with this functioning, body temperature gets raised causing fever. In such condition one can take a warm water bath to relieve stress and pain if any, and lower the fever . . .
>
> One should be cautious not to use very hot water lest the temperature [go] up. In order to avoid worsening of the fever, one should be cautious enough to keep the body hydrated by drinking plenty of fluids. This can include water and other drinks, which will enable maintenance of the electrolyte levels to the optimum level in the body and prevent dehydration. (Online Medicine Tips 2012)

My brother was extremely anemic, dehydrated, and depressed. After his diagnosis of cancer, he began to have nausea because his stress was now even greater. The combination of anemia and dehydration can be fatal if not taken care of immediately. As we began to nurture my brother with vitamins and healthy organic nutritious foods, he began to regain his appetite, and his immune system got stronger.

In *Alternative Medicine: The Definitive Guide* by Trivieri and Anderson:

> Immune enhancement therapies are frequently used by alternative physicians to treat cancer. A strong immune system is one of the keys to the delay and prevention of cancer, but the combination of poor nutrition and exposure to pollutants and natural toxins can cripple immune functions, as can the aging of the thymus gland. Immune enhancement

therapies seek to restore the immune system to optimum function so that the body can then subdue the cancer. In alternative medicine, this is accomplished without the side effects associated with conventional therapies. (2002, 600)

When a person with cancer is diagnosed, it is very important to treat the body with the alternative approach before the person's immune system is compromised through poisons from chemical medication, chemotherapy, and radiation. The most important thing to do is to enhance the immune system. When a person's body is strong, it's easy to fight any type of disease. Furthermore, the mind is not contaminated with negative input, fear, and the stress of undergoing the debilitating chemotherapy and radiation treatments traditionally prescribed by conventional medicine.

Every person whom I have known with different kinds of cancer has gone through a tremendous amount of stress for many different reasons. For example, my nephew was diagnosed with stomach cancer. After his father divorced his mother, he had extreme resentment towards him. My father was diagnosed with prostate cancer. He was devastated from the loss of his very young grandson through cancer. My brother was diagnosed with stomach cancer after having gone through a very difficult and painful divorce. A friend I knew was diagnosed with colon cancer after her husband had left her for a younger woman. Another friend was diagnosed with brain cancer after *her* only daughter had become a bad drug addict.

I could go on and on with stories of stress before cancer. From the people that I am mentioning in these examples, the only one who is still alive is my brother. The blueprint in all the cases I mentioned is obvious. This is what should make us wonder if cancer is stress that has been misdiagnosed and mishandled. Most of the people who have been diagnosed with cancer have no choice in the matter of their healing because of their lack of knowledge. Most people, especially in the

United States, are treated by conventional medicine. A few of them are strong and get rid of the stressors; others seek alternative treatments and get well. Both types of people are what we call "cancer survivors."

Now, we would all like to know what's going on with the cancer-cure delays from the research institutes. It has been decades since the research teams began collecting money through donations from different cancer groups to help them find a cure for this fatal disease. Do you think they really want to find the cure? Many cases of cancer cure have been accomplished by alternative approaches.

There is a lot of anger out there. The epidemic of cancer continues escalating uncontrollably. So many lives are being lost unnecessarily. We all know someone who is fighting cancer or has died from cancer. What can we do?

In a section on the website Healing Cancer Naturally (2015) titled "Why Alternative Cancer Treatment," the writers denounce cancer businesses and the cancer industry. In this section, they feature observations by cancer specialists and other individuals with concerns about this so-called "business" or "industry."

Below are some of the quotes from the website:

- *Oncology is one of the most profitable fields of medicine.* — Stephan Seeble, MD

- *We have a multi-billion dollar industry that is killing people, right and left, just for financial gain. Their idea of doing research is to see whether two doses of this poison are better than three doses of that poison.* — Glen A. Warner, MD, former head of the Inmunotherapy Department of the Tumor Institute under Orlis Wildermuth, MD

- *The field of US Cancer care is organized around a medical monopoly that [e]nsures a continuous flow of money to the pharmaceutical companies, medical technology firms, research institutes, and government agencies such as the* Food and Drug Administration (FDA), *and the* National Cancer Institute (NCI), *and quasi-public organizations such as the* American Cancer Society (ACS). — Ralph Moss, PhD, quoted by John Diamon, MD, and Lee Cowden, MD, in *Alternative Medicine, the Definitive Guide to Cancer.*

It's all about the money. We know that corruption is one of the biggest threats to all of us these days, especially the corruption of medical and pharmaceutical companies that affect our health directly. We need to wise up and take care of ourselves if we want to survive and have full lives.

As practitioners of holistic, natural medicine, we must be on a crusade to save lives, letting people know that there are natural, drug-less, and nonsurgical cures for almost every disease and that with the natural, holistic approach of prevention, there is a chance that you will hardly ever get sick again.

People need to understand that stress can be eliminated not with chemicals but by the power of our own minds. Our mission should be to teach people how to get rid of chronic stress by getting rid of the stressors and making the following decisions: to forgive, to accept, and to modify our lives and thoughts with positive thinking and a positive attitude. The body needs to be strengthened by good nutrition—i.e., by consuming organic foods without chemicals, pesticides, preservatives, and industrial pollutants. Exercise, vitamins, and supplements also play an important role in preventing cancer and curing cancer.

The availability and knowledge of alternative medicine has contributed to the health and well-being of many people already. Holistic medicine deals with mind, body, and spirit. It's up to each individual to search, make wise choices, and find ways to achieve a healthy life.

# TWENTY-ONE
## The Power of Emotion

In the first chapter of *Molecules of Emotion*, the book by Candace Pert that Bruce Lipton's comments had made essential reading for me, I knew that I had come to the right source for answers to my burning questions. In this case, I wouldn't have to trust my intuition quite so much: Pert begins the book with a lecture to a packed hall of people who had come to hear her because of her discoveries in neuroscience. All page numbers in parentheses without other information refer to this book (Pert 1997).

The lecture that begins the book continues in chapters 3 and 7 and concludes in chapter 9. The lecture is never dated, perhaps because it is a literary device telling us what she usually says when she meets the public—but in any case, because of the way she sums up her achievements, she wants us to bear them in mind as we read the story of her life as a scientist, her struggles to find the truth, and her concomitant struggle to publish it and be recognized for her work.

If the lecture was one she actually gave, it must have been given just before *Molecules of Emotion* was published in 1997, since she refers to Tom Wolfe's "recent" article in *Forbes* describing neuroscience as "the hottest field in the academic world" (14). That article appeared in 1996.

After describing her audience as the usual one—"alternative medicine practitioners," including "massage therapists, acupuncturists, chiropractors . . . people . . . marginalized for years, rarely taken seriously by the powers that be . . . the medical schools, insurance companies, the American Medical Association, the Food and Drug Administration . . ."—Pert goes on to predict the kinds of questions she will be asked when she's finished speaking by people trying to validate their theories and beliefs. "They have read about . . . how I have postulated a biochemical link between the mind and body, a new concept of the human organism as a communication network that redefines health and disease, empowering individuals with new responsibility, more control in their lives." Many seekers and philosophers have come, others merely because they are curious. Some have come because they need hope, and, where they are concerned, mainstream medicine has offered "no further answers, no treatment, no hope" (14–15).

Pert betrays the fact that she is using the lecture format as a way to present her ideas when she addresses the audience and "dear reader" all at once. But no matter; I, for one, needed this overview so that I wouldn't be distracted by all the adventures in her book (which made me wonder if academics and researchers were more proficient in skullduggery than the spies in novels of international intrigue or the arch-criminals in crime novels).

"First and foremost, I am a truth-seeker . . ." Pert declares. "My intention is to provide an understanding of the metaphors that express a new paradigm, metaphors that capture how inextricably united the body and the mind really are, and the role the emotions play in health and disease" (17). She then goes into the history of the separation of mind and body, pointing out that in conventional medicine, to bring "the mind too close to the body threatens the legitimacy of any particular illness, suggesting it may be imaginary, unreal, *unscientific*" (18).

This has been true, Pert says, since Descartes made "a turf deal with the Pope." In order to obtain the bodies he wanted for dissection, "he wouldn't have anything to do with the soul, the mind, or the emotions," which were under the jurisdiction of the Church at the time, "if he could claim the physical realm as his own." According to Pert, this created a gulf between science and religion that lasted for two centuries and is still with us today (18).

Pert goes on to say that the Cartesian era has been "dominated by reductionist methodology, which attempts to understand life by examining the tiniest pieces of it, and then extrapolating from the pieces to overarching surmises about the whole" (18).

She doesn't say so here, but it's obvious that all the specialization in science and medicine today is another manifestation of this atomization or reduction into tiny pieces. But Pert has a surprise in store for us. She's found a unifying principle that will put Humpty Dumpty back together again: "It is the emotions, I have come to see, that link mind and body. This more holistic approach complements the reductionist view, expanding it rather than replacing it, and offers a new way to think about health and disease . . ." (18–19).

In her book, Pert relies on the concept of "bodymind" and asserts that the "intelligence" of the bodymind will seek wellness without reliance on modern, high-tech medical interventions. Better than anyone, she knows how hard it is to gain acceptance for new ideas. She gives the example of Jesse Roth, who found insulin in one-celled animals and couldn't get his papers published because "everyone 'knew' that you needed a pancreas to make insulin." Roth was clinical director for the National Institutes of Health at the time and still had to put up with gibes like "you must not be washing your test tubes well enough" (19).

Pert suggests that science moves slowly for fear of making a mistake and often subjects new ideas to "nitpickingly intense scrutiny, if not outright rejection and revulsion, and getting them published becomes a Sisyphean labor" (19).

After a decade or more, the ideas that are preposterous to the establishment will become the status quo, and Pert sees that happening with her own ideas. Yet the foot-dragging on the part of the medical establishment has begun to be understood by the public, and she remarks on the anger she encounters as she crisscrosses the country from people who are "paying monstrous health care bills for often worthless procedures to remedy conditions that could have been prevented in the first place" (20).

After making this point, Pert begins an overview of her career from the time she discovered the opiate receptor (which made her famous) and a way to measure it. Anything that science can't measure doesn't exist, "which is why science refuses to deal with such 'nonthings' as the emotions, the mind, the soul, or the spirit" (21).

Like Lipton's, Pert's earthshaking discoveries began at the molecular level. Lipton's biggest breakthroughs came in his studies of cell membranes, while Pert focused on receptors and ligands. In the convenient dictionary she has provided at the back of the book, ligands are defined as "small molecules that specifically bind to a cellular receptor and in so doing convey an informational message to the cell" (350).

Again, I was amazed to learn that a typical neuron may have "millions of receptors on its surface" and that scientists can "isolate these receptors, determine their molecular weight, and eventually crack their chemical structure" (23).

There are three types of ligand: *neurotransmitters* such as acetylcholine, norepinephrine, dopamine, histamine, glycine, GABA, and serotonin; *steroids* such as testosterone, progesterone, and estrogen; and *peptides*, which comprise 95 percent of all ligands (25).

Yet endocrinologists with a special interest in understanding how hormones are able to act at a distance would not be found talking to pharmacologists: "So people in each field kept making parallel discoveries without understanding what these discoveries had in common" (29).

After describing Robert Jensen's studies with radioactive estrogen in 1960, Pert goes on to say, "Later, estrogen receptors, as well as receptors for testosterone and progesterone, were unexpectedly found in another organ, the brain, with amazing consequences for sexual identity. But that's a later part of our story" (29). Not too much later, I hoped!

Finally, Pert goes into the breakthrough that made her famous: "[the ramifications of the] discovery of the opiate receptor would extend into every field of medicine, uniting endocrinology, neurophysiology and immunology, and fueling a synthesis of behavior, psychology and biology. It was a discovery that touched off a revolution . . . But now my own story must begin" (30).

*Molecules of Emotion* could just as well have been called *The Candace Pert Story*. Just as Pert revolutionizes thinking about mind and body with her concept of bodymind, her discoveries in the laboratory are a function of her life: her relentless truth-seeking, her willingness to look at all sides of every problem and dissociate herself from the ideas and people who could have been useful to her career in favor of her intuitive feeling that these people and their ideas were not going far enough, and her love of life, which seemed to be a driving force as well.

Pert loved her work, and she loved the people who worked with her. Though happily married, she has no compunction about referring to a male who's working beside her in the laboratory as a "hunk." Reading her story, it's impossible not to share in the excitement of her life, her discoveries, her successful career strategies, the passion of her friendships, and her love of family.

There's a downside in that Pert doesn't seem to be aware when she's burning herself out (though the reader is) or when she's going too far in taking on her mentors and leaving bad feelings in her wake (though the reader is all too aware of her ambition and its recklessness). While taking the stage to give the lecture that, in installments, runs through the book, she tells us, "I'm not a rock star!," but she often behaves as if she were (16).

Moreover, Pert makes a statement in the way she dresses. She paints rainbows that begin in the hall outside her lab and bend around the door. Above all, she says what she thinks—and sometimes what she, or other people, shouldn't be thinking. She must have been a bit of a "loose cannon" for the heads of department at Johns Hopkins, the NIH, the "second biggest pharmaceutical company," the Cancer Institute, and the many other major institutions who employed her, hoping for the best. She behaved like a superstar of "the hottest of all fields," and it's hard to see her any other way.

A great part of the book has to do with the love-hate relationship between Pert and the man who ran the lab at Johns Hopkins, Solomon Snyder. He became her first sponsor in scientific research, the first to recognize the importance of her research and of the elegant experiments she designed, allocating a research assistant to help her when she was still only a grad student. However, he tried to prevent her continuing the opiate receptor research that she had pioneered precisely when she was about to have her breakthrough (37).

Where Snyder was concerned, gamesmanship was everything. And throughout her book, Pert makes the bitter point that all the political infighting meant nothing to her, even though she was pretty good at it. As a young researcher just starting out, she had a problem killing the animals that were involved in her studies—not just rats, but monkeys and other small creatures that were being ground up willy-nilly to advance our scientific knowledge. Before our eyes, she becomes a veteran researcher who is intimately aware that advances of the type she was seeking would require the sacrifice of the person she had always been in favor of the person she had to be. A more driven person would be hard to imagine.

So what did this inside story of careerism in science have to do with me and my small quest to find a few specific answers? Everything!

I had never been so fascinated by anything I had read about scientific achievement. The only example I could think of that could engage my emotions or my sense of justice this completely was the battle of Tesla versus Edison late in the nineteenth century—the battle between a visionary who also happened to be a great scientist and promoter (Tesla) and a great scientist who happened to be an even greater self-publicist (Edison).

This was something like the same kind of struggle, except that Candace Pert was destined to run into one self-aggrandizing manipulator after another all her life. Those whom she considered her greatest allies would lose their nerve when they had to stand up for her or for what was right. Famous figures in science who had made their names in related research would jump at the chance to meet her and then marvel that they were able to make her cry. But why did the story of her uphill struggle make such a difference to me, working away in the dark in a remote little town in a huge, empty place like West Texas?

My biggest problem in doing what I still called "my research" was the fact that I was collecting an emotional response from all the women I interviewed, a sense of something they had been thinking when they were pregnant. Their recollections about what had actually happened could not be quantified in any way. Even if their intuition was telling them, as mine had told me, that gender identity had something to do with strong feelings about the desired sex of the baby they were carrying, it would be impossible to interest scientists in doing a study based on such intuitions—any intuitions.

Long before I'd ever heard of Candace Pert or read a book about quantum mechanics or the possibility of my subconscious being influenced by a kind of blueprint that I couldn't see or grasp with my mind—but that was somehow real to the cells of my body—I was telling myself "forget it." I couldn't picture myself explaining something like that to an intelligent child such as my second daughter or to my first, when she was a child, much less to a doctor sitting across from me in his private office, sworn to honor my confidences and thus unable to make me ridiculous for expressing such thoughts or even for harboring them.

Yet if . . . If I had been right all along, and someone was able to assert that yes, there was something in my intuition, and there were many factors that made it likely that my intuition would be borne out eventually by studies that would be accepted by scientists the way they had accepted E=mc². This is why my heart filled with hope when I read a line like "my intuition told me that the opiate receptor was there" (54). Still, it made me uneasy to read other examples of Pert's intuition: "In my heart of hearts, I knew that the only payment for the fast track would be a migraine at the end of the day, or perhaps a coronary bypass before the age of fifty" (121).

She missed the coronary by seventeen years, but her intuition was right on track.

Pert is not only honest about her findings and about her dealings with great men who could sometimes reach self-serving decisions at the expense of humanity, make personal use of their discoveries, or be small-minded in other ways; she is honest about herself:

> While I was working out the kinks, Sol got some of the other people in the lab to try out the new technique . . . Instant Eureka! Immediately, Sol switched all his postdocs over to our method and directed them to use it to scan for receptors for all the known brain chemicals. When I showed signs of getting possessive about my hard-won methodology, Sol ordered Adele to show everyone the ropes—how to make the 'magic membranes,' as I called them, when to mix the test tubes vigorously, how to filter—all the little tricks of the trade that Adele and I had evolved to guarantee good data every day. (80)

The lab work Pert was doing has universal interest. Many laboratories and many brilliant minds from all the major industrial powers are "going for the gold." In other words, the field is inherently exciting because what these scientists find will affect us all. It will change medical practice (and already has in forward-looking parts of the world—not necessarily in the United States!); it will change what we should ask of our leaders and how we should plan our lives; it will influence how we take care of ourselves and our families by changing ways of thinking that are now causing us stress or doing overt damage to our bodies; it will change the way we seek medical or health advice and the way we educate our children.

Yet at every turn, the citizens who have most to gain from breakthroughs like the kind that Pert was almost routinely making are being cheated of the benefits of most of the research. Even when their results are extraordinary, the scientists who are risking the most and going it alone have to scratch and claw their way into the kinds of publications that will enable their findings to be taken seriously.

As for the commercial interests that often sponsor cutting-edge research, it would appear from Pert's book (which reads like an exposé at times) that the main problem humanity has in the area of pure science is the same problem we face in the areas of climate change (because of the vested interests of energy corporations) and geopolitical turmoil (because of the military-industrial-political complex). Especially where Big Pharma is concerned, there are right results and wrong results before laboratory investigations are ever undertaken. The big money that awaits investigators large and small is for finding what they're supposed to find, not for finding the truth. As Bruce Lipton does in his book, Pert shows convincingly that the medical establishment has a vested interest in treating allopathically (with pharmaceuticals) in spite of the huge incidence of iatrogenic illness in this country (illness caused mostly by drug side effects or interactions, which is currently our country's third leading cause of death . . . or its fourth, depending on your source of information).

Disturbing as these conclusions may be, *Molecules of Emotion* is not a "downer." It is not a depressing book to read. Discoveries of scientific truth are thrilling by their very nature, and when they take place, the reader wants to celebrate right along with Pert and her colleagues. By the same token, we share her anger and frustration when she is prevented from doing work that has the potential to make life better for millions of people. Thus do bureaucratic or self-serving political decisions condemn long-suffering people to suffer more and suffer longer. Sadly, the political aspect of Pert's struggle needn't have happened in the first place without the "old-boy network" that seems to have been in place long before she arrived on the scene and that shows no signs of breaking up in spite of the appearance of more and more female researchers.

This is the story of a rebel, then, but it will have particular relevance for female scientists.

Just before the epilogue at the end of the book, Pert sums up the core beliefs that have seen her through the fight: "The heart of science is feminine. In its essence science has very little to do with competition, control, separation—all qualities that have come to be associated with science in its male-dominated, twentieth-century form. The science that I have come to know and love is unifying, spontaneous, intuitive, caring—a process more akin to surrender than domination" (315).

Surrender to honest emotions, that is, while we hold our left-brained dreams of power and winning at bay. Pert's last words to us are as follows: "Science at its most exalted is a truth-seeking endeavor, which encompasses the values of cooperation and communication, based on trust—trust in ourselves and in one another" (315).

So much for the life of Candace Pert, which was lived largely out of the limelight, serving these values. Toward the end of her life, when she was much in demand as a public speaker, she went to the platform in flowing robes with "lots of purple," holding forth on alternative medicine. She confided that her life had become starkly two-sided: on the East Coast, she was a relentless seeker of scientific truth who never turned back from research problems that demanded rigorous analysis and great patience, but she had a huge appetite for "Californoid" therapies and techniques for self-improvement as well. The whole last third of her book is a long treatise on the virtues of alternative methods in medicine and healing, many of which may be unfamiliar to the general reader.

Nevertheless, as we have come to know her, these dalliances on the fringe of behavioral exploration haven't changed a bit of her commitment to the hard science that always formed the core of her commitments and her love of life. She was so completely at home as a truth-seeking investigator that both of her marriages were collaborations. Pert shared her life completely with the men she loved, just as she wanted to share the glory for her successes with other researchers and the meaning of her research with all humanity.

Her struggle with Sol Snyder deserves the huge place she gives it in her life story. It is probably true that by going public about her quarrel with him and about the way he had cut her out from the credit she deserved for her discovery of the opiate receptor, she cost him the Nobel Prize. She wouldn't have done what she did if Snyder had been willing to mention her as one of the co-discoverers.

It may still be true that women are being discriminated against, as she was, and that recognition for their very real achievements in science is being prevented. Yet perhaps the members of the "old-boy network" have learned something from taking on a first-rate scientist and committed truth-seeker like Candace Pert. The whole story should be read and savored by all the women who are working in science—and perhaps it has been, though her influence is sure to have been eroded by the heart disease that claimed her life.

Of course, the way Pert describes the progression from the highest academic standing to maverick status (as a champion of alternative medicine) was dear to my heart, as it was with Bruce Lipton. I was coming to understand that I was on the side of the mavericks. I was once again confirmed in my intuitive distrust of pharmaceutical remedies and convinced that they are almost never "good for what ails you," even if they can alleviate symptoms for a time.

In the short subchapter devoted to "The Mind-Body Connection: Emotion-Carrying Peptides" (140–41), Pert spoke to me directly and provided the exact answers I had been looking for. In discovering that there were many possible hookups to facilitate mind-body connections, she was also discovering what was getting communicated:

> For example, the receptors for sex hormones that had been unexpectedly identified in the brain and then ignored for many years were clearly the mechanism through which testosterone and estrogen, if released into the fetus during pregnancy, could determine neuronal connections in the brain and permanently affect the sexual identity of the child. John Money, the famous Johns Hopkins psychiatrist, had shown that female fetuses exposed to testosterone-like steroid hormones (aberrantly produced by their pregnant mothers' adrenal glands) were more likely to become tomboys and avoid dolls! (140)

Pert goes on to describe "additional nerve hookups" that could now be discovered "thanks to the invention of new biochemical tools with which to examine them . . . Neuropeptides could be found not only in the rows of nerve ganglia on either side of the spine, but in the end organs themselves . . . New peptide-containing groups of neuronal cell bodies in the brain called 'nuclei,' the sources of most brain-to-body and body-to-brain hookups, are now being elaborated upon every day" (140).

Pert's examples of these hookups are numerous and lead us to expect that more will be discovered as long as scientists are interested in finding them—or monetarily rewarded for doing so. One unusual finding explains the unusual hookup between human sexuality and the eliminative functions (peeing and pooping). These studies, which are by Rita Valentino at the University of Pennsylvania, help us to understand how a loop between the nucleus of Barrington in the hindbrain "sends axons containing the neuropeptide CRF down through the vagus nerve all the way to the most distant part of the large intestine, near the anus." Then, through "a short neuronal pathway (called a 'projection') . . . the locus coeruleus is hooked up: the norepinephrine-containing source of the 'pleasure pathway,' which is also very high in opiate receptors" (140–41).

Is it any wonder, Pert asks rhetorically, "that toilet training is loaded with emotional stuff! Or that people get into some unusual sexual practices involving bathroom behaviors! Clearly, the classical physiologists had grossly underestimated the complexity and scope of the neurochemistry and neuroanatomy of the autonomic nervous system" (141). Pert concludes what was, for me, the most important revelation in her book by imagining how Freud would have felt that his theories had been vindicated by these molecular confirmations: "The body is the unconscious mind" (141).

(I think it should be noted again for emphasis that scientists use "subconscious" and "unconscious" interchangeably. In fact, Pert wrote a book titled *The Body is the Subconscious Mind*. This blurring may confuse people for whom English is a second language, but scientists are clearly comfortable with it.)

Furthermore, "repressed traumas caused by overwhelming emotion can be stored in a body part." My emotions when I was pregnant could not have been more overwhelming. I would have given anything to have my marriage restored through a kind of hereditary gift that would end my apparent uselessness as a wife and mother: "The new work suggests there are almost infinite pathways for the conscious mind to access—and modify—the unconscious mind and body, and also provides an explanation for a number of phenomena that the emotional theorists have been considering" (141).

One revelation followed another in the subsequent subchapter, "The Mind in the Body: Filtering, Storing, Learning, Remembering, Repressing": "Using neuropeptides as the cue, our bodymind retrieves or represses emotions and behaviors . . . I'd say that the fact that memory is encoded or stored at the receptor level means that memory processes are emotion-driven and unconscious (but, like other receptor-mediated processes, can sometimes be made conscious)" (143).

And in the subchapter "State-Dependent Memory and Altered Consciousness: Our Peptides at Work": "Clearly, just as drugs can affect what we remember, neuropeptides can act as internal ligands to shape our memories as we are forming them, and put us back in the same frame of mind when we need to retrieve them. This is learning. In fact, we have shown that the hippocampus of the brain, without which we cannot learn anything new, is a nodal point for neuropeptide receptors, containing virtually all of them" (144–45).

In the following subchapter, "Creating Our Own Reality, Realizing Our Own Expectations," Pert gives examples drawn from the many questions she was evidently asking of friends and fellow researchers about ways that the conscious mind can help to filter a "deluge of sensory input" so that we can "pay attention to what our bodymind deems the most important pieces of information and ignore the others" (146).

Pert gives the example of Norman Cousins (the man who defeated cancer with laughter), who altered blood flow to "a broken elbow, which he had suffered while playing tennis, and got back on the court in record time simply by focusing for twenty minutes each day on increasing the blood flow through the injured joint, after his physician explained that poor blood supply to the elbow was why injuries to this joint healed slowly" (146–47).

By now, I understood enough to realize that traditional medicine was only equipped to tell us, "this is why you suffer," not to tell us how to do something about suffering. Healing and medicine have never been so far apart as they are today in the country where "greed is good."

When she confronted the cancer establishment that blocked her ideas for new treatment, Pert claimed that this was her first exposure to "the intransigence of old-paradigm thinking," but we who have been following her story know very well that it was not. Again and again, she came up against outmoded paradigms based on the Newtonian model. In her book, she had been identifying them all along. In some ways, it seems she may have been blind to the forces that were arrayed against her. Or maybe the force of her will and the desire to be vindicated by the establishment were something she couldn't share with others. Anyway, she shares so much personal, emotionally charged information with her readers that it seems narrow-minded and carping to ask for more.

Even so, sadly, this sense of someone waking up to the awful realities that have hamstrung our science and marginalized the hard work of female investigators effected the whole progression of Pert into New Age therapies and even into the alternative medicine that had done so much to inspire me.

The women who kept answering my questions—thinking back to when they were pregnant, how they felt at the time, and the deep desires that they had no idea they were sharing with their unborn child—these women would never be supported in trying to understand what had happened to their children by people like Norman Cousins. Their voices could not introduce measurable quantities of anything into the argument. No matter that they might grow to understand their intuition, respect it more, and even respect mine—or perhaps someday read words in a book by me or by someone who had the same personal experiences, many years of research, and would be qualified to talk about such matters—no one was going to stop the "old paradigm thinking" of somehow blaming LGBTQ children born with gender identity issues for expressing behavior that shatters the old paradigms that have sanctified the heterosexual couple. Nor do they acknowledge the rightful existence of any other behavioral standard. This condemns the rest of us to the mindless creation of misery, and there isn't a parent on the planet, no matter how miserable, who wishes his or her child to be miserable.

In a way, as she went on the lecture circuit, stumped for alternative medicine for a good part of each year, and then went back to her laboratory and saw peptide T (which she had developed with husband number two, Michael Ruff) go down to defeat after defeat, I can't help but feel that Pert's emotional life was bottled up somehow. The recognition she deserved, which would have translated into funding, which in turn would have translated into new discoveries—discoveries that might have changed the course of our thinking for generations to come by proposing a new paradigm, acceptable even in our classrooms and inspiring to the young—wasn't going to come. The old-boy system was going to prevail. But even though she had lost hope, she hadn't lost her belief in humanity or her belief that the right ideas would win out in the end. AIDS would be defeated along with many other scourges of mankind. She had done all she could, and though she couldn't have known it—except in glimmers of intuition—her own time was short (159–79).

Having read about the zero-point field and heard similar despair and similar dreams of eventual triumph in the thinking of many other warriors for truth in science and medicine, I realized that though Pert had answered many of my questions—about the function of the bodymind, the way the limbic system (and really all the systems of the body) were in contact, the way the body was the subconscious mind, and the way the mind could negotiate with the body—because she chose not to consider the field and was in other respects a traditional scientist, she put very little emphasis on the subconscious as a source of knowledge for the mind and on the field, through the mediation of quantum theory, as the source of reality for the subconscious.

Because of its far narrower function as a switching station, the brain manages the messages of the bodymind and all the emotions being collected at various nodal outposts, but the mind often fails to accurately judge the content of these messages. The brain is vulnerable to fear and survival pressures that never afflict the subconscious mind in the slightest.

When we are depressed, for example, our brains have difficulty processing reality and begin to create a fantasy reality whose terms are easier to understand. We're defining the terms of our success and derive some comfort from this illusion, but our concept can get way out of alignment with the messages that are being received and stored by the subconscious mind as long as we live. So, in essence, we live in fear of ourselves and begin to think of the death of our conscious minds as the death of the reality that has created us.

# TWENTY-TWO
## A Higher Consciousness

In the next big book of my life, I would understand a source of joy in the unknown that had often been a source of fear. Every word in this book—*Power vs. Force*, by Dr. David Hawkins—seemed to speak to me with hope and inspired me to continue in my quest for truth. Page numbers given without other information refer only to this book.

The more I took Dr. Hawkins's words to heart, the more peace and joy I found. I had to look no further. I had discovered a treasure trove; I hadn't stopped looking for truth, far from it, but I was more open to everything I was able to find. As Hawkins states, "The truth of one's Self can be discovered in everyday life. To live with care and kindness is all that is necessary. The rest reveals itself in due time. The commonplace and God are not distinct" (2012, xliv).

Hawkins devised the Map of Consciousness and named his teachings "Devotional Nonduality." He claims that they embody the following core principles: "kindness and compassion to everything and everyone (including oneself), humility, forgiveness, simplicity, lovingness as a way of being, reverence for all of life, devotion to Truth and surrender to God" (xxxix). Who would quarrel with such a program? Certainly not I. My hopes couldn't have been raised any higher.

Since I started reading in English, I'd worried that meanings were escaping me. In reading Hawkins, there was no such thing. But because of the book's lucidity and the way it goes down like a long drink of water, it will be difficult to follow it chapter by chapter. Every line of Hawkins's book is quotable. He doesn't use long sentences. Nor does he spend a long time dwelling on a single aspect of his method or a couple of key ideas. This time, while the book is fresh in my mind (I've just reread it yet again), I'm merely going to touch on the things I took from it, the ideas it gave me that were life-changing, and the way they related to my readings of Wayne Dyer, Andrew Weil, John Sarno, Lynne McTaggart, Bruce Lipton, and Candace Pert.

Hawkins's ideas build in complexity to the end. Putting the book down, I knew that I would carry these ideas for the rest of my life and that, because of them, I would never see the world the same way. The purpose of my life had changed. The meaning of it had changed. My way of thinking had changed.

For me, Hawkins's ideas were a bridge between the zero-point field and the molecular and neurotransmitter work of the biologists I'd been reading—a bridge between physics and physiology. And also between science and religion, something that had troubled me from the beginning of my studies!

Hawkins weighs in with the claim that had already attracted me to his book: that to understand "one simple thing in depth" was to expand our capacity for "comprehending the nature of the universe and of life itself" (xxi). For this, he has devised a scale of consciousness that was found to coincide with that devised by Aldous Huxley in his *Perennial Philosophy*, a book that I had already read (xxii). Later in my studies, I was directed to Ken Wilber to help chart spiritual progress. I only mention him here to dispel the idea that I was completely uncritical in my acceptance of everything that Hawkins had to say. I was trying to learn new things, but in so doing, I wasn't throwing out everything I knew or abandoning my ability to think or question.

Hawkins warns us that having a ready reference to know everything about anything like this might create a "paradigm shock"—a good way of describing the almost miraculous powers that one was assuming. Yet long experience and many thousands of tests will, he assures us, confirm these new abilities of ours. He goes on to describe the way our intuition will function to make our understanding ever clearer: "Each time we return to comment on an example, greater comprehension will occur" (xxvi). Well, this is certainly the way the world of the mind ought to operate, but was *my* mind up to the job? Anyway, I had to know, and I was eager to turn all the pages of this book, hoping for the best.

Finally, in his own introduction to the book, Hawkins asserts that "man's dilemma—now and always—has been that he misidentifies his own intellectual artifacts as reality" (xlix). Here was further substantiation of what I had learned from Lipton and Pert: the brain creates the reality it needs to have in order to be satisfied with the reality of the world as perceived by our senses and described to us by our fellows and, of course, first and foremost by our parents ("self-referential thinking"). I was by now well aware of the human capacity for fooling ourselves and felt that I had done a good bit of it myself—or I wouldn't have found myself in West Texas married to a man who hadn't the slightest interest in my welfare or the welfare of my child by him.

Hawkins goes on to say that the "fatal faults of all thought systems have been, primarily: (1) failure to differentiate between subjective and objective; (2) disregard of the limitation of context inherent in basic design and terminology; (3) ignorance of the nature of consciousness itself; and (4) misunderstanding of the nature of causality" (l-li). Furthermore, he asserts a bit later on the same page that "the basic law of the universe is economy. The universe does not waste a single quark;

all serves a purpose and fits into a balance—there are no extraneous events" (li). Well, how could there be? The one fish missing from the school might have been the one which first perceived danger. This seemed to be a restatement of the principle I had heard somewhere: "everything serves."

Hawkins's conclusion is stated in language that was so beautiful to my ears that I found myself reading and rereading this section, waiting for my astonishment to subside: "From the human record, we may note that answers never arise from identifying so-called 'causes' in the world. Instead, it is necessary to identify the conditions that underlie ostensible causes . . . the observable world is a world of effects" (li). These glorious words resolve in a promise that we will, and must, make a "quantum leap" in consciousness that will be marked by a "sudden expansion of context and understanding . . . an inner experience of relief, joy, and awe. All who have had such an experience feel afterward that the universe has granted them a precious gift" (lv).

Finally, I had made it to chapter 1 (of part 1), titled "Tools." But I was still being stopped in my tracks by summary statements that astonished me. On the first page: "Kinesiology exposed, for the first time, the intimate connection between the mind and body, revealing that the mind 'thinks' with the body itself" (59). Then, somewhat later: "Medicine had forgotten that it was an art, and that science was merely a tool of that art" (60). Finally, Hawkins identifies the "last great barrier to human knowledge [as] the investigation of the nature of consciousness itself" (61).

Later, "by identifying subjective and objective as the same, we are able to transcend the constraints of the concept of time," such as our ideas of seeming causality, I supposed (62). Then, Hawkins directly answered a question I had been asking myself ever since coming to the United States: "Living things all react to what is life-supportive and what is not; this is the fundamental mechanism of survival. Inherent in all life forms is the ability to detect change and react correctively—thus, trees become smaller at higher elevation as the oxygen in the air becomes scarcer. Human protoplasm is far more sensitive than that of a tree" (63).

From here, Hawkins goes into a technical discussion of attractor fields, of fields of dominance, of critical point analysis, and of causality. Instead of logical progression (reasoning from observed sequences in nature to an ultimate principle), Hawkins will be operating from another paradigm, one based on the work of David Bohm, Rupert Sheldrake, and Karl Pribram: from attractor patterns to operants to observable events. In essence, as I understood it, we were at last imagining the universe as a creation of God, and this intuition was rewarded in the last line of the chapter, in which he says, "Genius . . . commonly attributes the source of creative leaps of awareness to that basis of all consciousness, which has traditionally been called Divinity" (71–72).

At last, my heart and mind and spirit were being swept along by the same words, and I felt strongly that I was being healed in some way.

But why take it on my authority? In Hawkins's "Map of Consciousness," he has written a short essay on each of the stages of awareness, from the dimmest beginnings with "Shame" to "Joy," "Peace," and "Enlightenment." Each step on the way is identified by a process: Shame, for example, is identified by "Elimination," the latter three by "Transfiguration," "Illumination," and "Pure Consciousness."

It is possible to quote anything at all from each essay and have it perfectly serve to illustrate that particular state. In turn, then, we can quote: "Driven, intolerant" individuals motivated by Shame (level 20) are "moral extremists who form vigilante groups, projecting their own unconscious shame onto others whom they then feel justified in righteously attacking or killing" (98–99). The behavior of lynch mobs and serial killers comes to mind.

Guilt (level 30) can be characterized by the behavior of "sin and salvation merchants obsessed with punishment" and with "either acting out their own guilt or projecting it onto others" (99–100).

Apathy (level 50) is identified with people who have "lost the will to live." These hopeless people "stare blankly, unresponsive to stimuli, until their eyes stop tracking and there is not even enough energy left to swallow proffered food" (100).

In Grief (level 75) "one sees sadness everywhere." It is as though "sorrow were the price of life" (100–01).

Fear (level 100) is healthy in response to danger, but when it becomes one's focus, it is fed by the "endless fearful events of the world" (101–02).

Desire (level 125) is "insatiable because it is an ongoing energy field," so the "satisfaction of one desire is immediately replaced by unsatisfied desire for something else" (102–03).

Anger (level 150) "is exemplified by irritable, explosive people who are oversensitive to slights and become 'injustice collectors'" (103–04).

As for Pride (level 175): "The whole problem of denial is one of Pride" (104–05).

Power first appears at the level of Courage (level 200). "This is where productivity begins" (105–06).

Neutrality (level 250) is marked by "a confident capability to live in the world" (106–07).

Willingness (level 310): "The willing . . . will take any job when they have to or create a career or self-employment for themselves" (108).

With Acceptance (level 350), a major transformation has taken place "with the recognition that one is oneself the source and creator of the experience of one's life" (109–10).

Reason (level 400) is not in itself a guide to truth, as "all philosophic arguments sound convincing on their own" (110–11).

Love (level 500) comes from the heart and "has the capacity to lift others and accomplish great feats because of its purity of motive" (111–13).

With Joy (level 540), there is a "capacity for enormous patience and the persistence of a positive attitude in the face of prolonged adversity . . . The hallmark of this state is compassion" (113–14).

Peace (level 600) is "extremely rare. Everything is connected to everything else by a Presence whose power is infinite, exquisitely gentle, yet rock solid" (114–15).

Above level 700 is "the level of the great ones of history who originated the spiritual patterns that multitudes have followed throughout the ages." Mother Teresa calibrated at 710, and the Indian saint Ramana Maharshi at 720. Levels 700 to 1,000 indicate various enlightened states in which the complete non-duality of Oneness has been attained. Lord Krishna, Lord Buddha, and the Lord Jesus Christ all calibrate at 1,000 (115–16).

Hawkins concludes his discussion of the state of consciousness on the hopeful note that because changes in energy level are logarithmic, "individual choice can have a mighty effect . . . transforming both one's life and one's effect on the world at large" (123).

I felt myself being transformed as I read along.

The high state that people seek by whatever means is, in fact, the Experience field of their own consciousness (Self). If they are spiritually unsophisticated and lack a context with which to comprehend the experience, they believe it is created by something "'out there' (such as a guru, music, drugs, lover, and so forth). . . . All that has actually happened is that . . . they have experienced their inner reality" (127).

Hawkins continues to describe the usefulness of his method to greatly shorten the time it takes to do industrial and scientific research, especially materials research, giving the example of Thomas Edison's test of over sixteen hundred materials before he struck on tungsten for his light bulb (131). He goes on to describe uses in product development, scientific inquiry, and medical science. Further uses are carefully described in theology, epistemology, and philosophy. Finally, its uses in everyday critical point analysis create a situation in which "sheep's clothing need no longer hide the wolf" (131–37).

Exhaustively, as in all his analyses, Hawkins details the possibilities of understanding for current and historic events; health research; criminal justice and police work (especially in crimes where there are no witnesses); timesaving by means of statistics and methodology; politics and government; commerce; science and research; clinical work; and education (140–46). In the final section on spirituality, he says, "Simple kindness to one's self and all that lives is the most powerful transformational force of all. It produces no backlash, has no downside, and never leads to loss or despair" (150–51).

In discussing the source of power, Hawkins shows how lives that are dedicated to the creation and embodiment of beauty (the lives of great artists, for example) lead to longevity and vigor. And at this point, Hawkins goes into a thorough discussion of the theories of Bohm, Sheldrake, and the creators of chaos theory, leading to the realization of "what mystics have claimed for centuries: that the universe is indeed coherent, unified, and organized around unifying patterns" (160).

In part 2 of his book, titled "Work," Hawkins deconstructs the world using the parameters he has introduced earlier. For example, he gives us a list of 140 words in columns showing strong attractor patterns and weak attractor patterns: Cheerful . . . Manic; Fertile . . . Luxuriant; Loyal . . . Chauvinistic; Timeless . . . Faddish; and so on (168–69). He adds, "The universe holds its breath as we choose, instant by instant, which pathway to follow; for the universe, the very essence of life itself, is highly conscious" (170). Furthermore, "Every act or decision you make that supports life, supports all of life, including your own. The ripples we create return to us" (170–71).

Further wise words follow about surviving success and achieving physical health through power: "a basic dictum of nonlinear dynamics and attractor research [is that] attractors create context" (229). In this chapter, Hawkins tackles the problem of stress, concluding that all stress is originated internally by one's attitudes. Here, he discusses a book he wrote with Linus Pauling called *Orthomolecular Psychiatry*, which was ignored by the scientific community of the time (June 1973), along with a later paper, because, according to Hawkins, "there was still no paradigm to give it credibility" (233).

In his chapter on wellness and the disease process, Hawkins insightfully states that "relatively few people are genuinely committed to peace as a realistic goal. In their private lives, people prefer being 'right' at whatever cost to their relationships or themselves. A self-justified positionality is the real enemy of peace" (241).

In the third and final part of his book, titled "Meaning," Hawkins goes back to explain in depth the collective unconscious of Carl Jung, which I immediately saw as another way of describing the field as I had read about in McTaggart's book. Many of his observations had a familiar ring: "the entire manifest universe is its own simultaneous expression and experience of itself" (249).

Never mind that other reading had made these ideas familiar to me; never had they been explained so lucidly.

In the discussion of the evolution of consciousness, Hawkins makes the astounding statement that "there is nothing that the mind believes that is not fallacious at a higher level of awareness. The mind, then, identifies with its content . . . in fact, it is only experiencing experiencing itself" (266).

Hawkins continues:

> From thinking that we "are" our minds, we begin to see that we "have" minds, and that it is the mind that has thoughts, beliefs, feelings, and opinions. Eventually, we may arrive at the insight that all our thoughts are merely borrowed from the great database of consciousness and were never really our own to begin with . . . As we place less value on such passing notions, they lose their power to dominate us, and

we experience progressive freedom of, as well as from, the mind. This, in turn, ripens into a new source of pleasure; fittingly the pleasure of existence itself matures as one ascends the scale of consciousness. (267)

So many things have been resolved! For me, anyway, I finally had the sense of a unity of life and spirit that Hawkins not only talks about but also illustrates as a scientific, molecular, and emotional reality. The concept of one God had taken on new meaning: one energy bathing the universe in love, resolving all the divisive forces in the world, all the battles, and all the confrontations with the power of loving awareness. Never again could I be against some people and for others; I was only for humanity. There was nothing to be against.

The better I understood life, the more it resembled a kind of endless unfolding (as in David Bohm's model) or an endless flowering (as in the model proposed by the Buddha). To live in such a universe with the power to observe this unfolding was the very meaning of "to be blessed." Where people had been deformed by their beliefs, the reality of the subconscious was at work in the quiet of night to restore their thinking; where mistaken ideas were transmitted to our young, as I had transmitted them to my darling daughter, the force of God's love was showing me the meaning of my daughter's way of growing and changing. If only I would stop prejudging the result of her unfolding and see the beauty of it, I would see God's grandeur and I would understand that there are no mistakes in his creation.

The Garden of Earthly Delights is not full of sensuality, as the painter Bosch conceived it in the Middle Ages; it is full of innocent beauty and sacred purpose. And our highest purpose is to delight our Creator and praise his name. It is most fitting, then, that David Hawkins ends everything he writes with the Latin saying *Gloria in Excelsis Deo!*

# TWENTY-THREE
## My Mother's Healing

I earned my bachelor's degree in holistic natural medicine on April 23, 2012, at sixty-seven years of age. The study of holistic medicine now enabled me to help friends and family with health problems. I never charged for my help; in other ways, my help was different from a traditional doctor's, but thanks to my training and the success of my recommendations, I gained confidence in my abilities as a health practitioner. Of course, I had sensed all along that I was on the right track in health matters by taking my own advice. In the way Americans refer to people like me, I "practiced what I preached."

In mid-September 2013, I was awakened by one of those frightening early-morning phone calls. One of my sisters was calling from South America to tell me that my mother had been hospitalized and was not doing very well. My mother was ninety-two at the time. Obviously, her age was a big concern, but I was also aware that, several years before, she'd been diagnosed with type 2 diabetes. She had been admitted to the hospital after being found unconscious in her room from an insulin overdose. After her insulin injection, she hadn't eaten enough and said she hadn't been hungry.

I told my sister to keep me posted about her condition. As time went by, my mother just kept getting worse. The doctors at the hospital in Ecuador immediately took care of her insulin problem, but they were also performing all kinds of tests to see what else was wrong with her, and they were already treating her with several medications.

A week later, one of the doctors at the hospital told my sister that my mother had thyroid cancer, so she was being prepared for treatments. I knew this was the usual thing in conventional medicine, but I was even more apprehensive than usual because of my studies. As I saw it, a person who is treated with alternative medicine right after the cancer diagnosis has a better chance of healing and surviving cancer than someone exposed to chemotherapy and radiation treatments. This is so because the immune system is debilitated by these treatments and the body is forced to fight the disease with weakened defenses.

The next day, I called a sister of mine who lives in the United States, and we decided to go see my mother. Family members told us to bring clothing for a funeral because my mother's condition was very bad. I left Texas in the first week of October 2013. My sister was waiting for me at the Quito airport. Since my flight from Texas arrived at midnight, we decided to spend the night near the airport and drive to the city first thing in the morning.

As we arrived at the hospital the next morning, it was heartbreaking to see my mother in such terrible shape. It's not enough to describe what I saw on her face as pain and hopelessness. She was on several medications and had lost her appetite. As a consequence, she had lost a lot of weight. The only thing that was going into her stomach at this time was an array of different medications and different chemicals. I found myself thinking, *How can anyone survive on chemicals alone?*

When my sister and I got to the hospital, it was about 10:00 a.m. My sister and I were in the room with my mother for almost seven hours, enough time to observe all aspects of her care. I noticed that when hospital workers brought the patients their meals, they put down the tray and left the room. If the patient ate the food that had been brought, fine, but if not, they didn't seem too concerned about it. I had seen this kind of thing happening in the United States as well. Yet when medications are brought, the hospital workers in both countries (and maybe all over the world) stick around to make sure that everything is taken.

By three in the afternoon, I felt we had seen enough. I told my sister that we needed to take my mother home. The main reason was the difficulty of starting her on alternative care. We sought out the doctor who was in charge of my mother's care to request her release from the hospital. Because of the previous experiences with my father and brother, I knew that my mother needed to be at home for us to care for her properly. When I spoke to my mother, she wanted to go home also. If she was going to die, we all wanted her to die peacefully at home, surrounded by her children.

I have to give thanks to the doctors in my country for being so willing to please their patients' families. I have not known them to interfere with patients' wishes or with the wishes of their loved ones. My mother's doctor ordered her release from the hospital immediately. It took two hours to get her discharge instructions and all the other paperwork ready, plus two paper sacks full of medication.

One of the nurses who was taking care of my mother's release needed her social security number; I did not know where she had that information, but knowing that she knew the number by memory, we asked her. My mother gave us the first two numbers; she then paused and thought very hard. Very sadly, she told us that she couldn't remember any more numbers. Big tears rolled down from her eyes. Until that moment, she had always been lucid. Finally, at about 5:00 p.m., everything was ready, and she could be taken home.

My mother had been given a medication that is used to protect cells in radiation therapy. This medication had been given to her the day before our arrival to prepare her for that kind of treatment. The side effects had been tremendous. My mother was confused and had weakness and muscle pain, among other things. When we got ready to begin the trip home, the nurses who were assisting my mother on the wheelchair, my sister, a sister-in-law, and I had a terrible time getting her into the car. Her muscle pain was excruciating. Back home, her bedroom was upstairs, so we had to pay a security guard to carry her up to it. All the way to the bedroom, my mother was moaning and complaining of pain. It's emotionally draining to see a loved one in such distress.

This was the beginning of my mother's holistic treatment—an amalgamation of mind, body, and spirit.

With the knowledge from my studies of holistic medicine and my previous experiences with my father's cancer, my brother's cancer, and my own heart attack, I knew there was a natural cure for almost every malady; with this fact in hand, I was sure that we could make my mother well again.

My mother had lived for many years near an area long renowned for longevity—Vilcabamba, Ecuador. This little town on the slopes of the Andes Mountains is one of the three spots in the world where people live exceptionally long lives. Mention of this small town brings back memories of an elderly man who told us stories when we were small children. Some of my siblings and I spent time during the summer with the daughters of my second uncle, who was the pharmacist and the doctor in that town. This elderly man's name was Mr. Carpio. He was interviewed and photographed at the age of 123 by *National Geographic* magazine.

Mr. Carpio said, "Oh, to be 108 again! . . . I would not like to be young again," he explained, "but if I could take 15 years from my age—wonderful!" (Leaf 1973, 114). The townspeople claimed that he finally died at the age of 132, so it's not presumptuous of me to say that my father died too early at eighty-nine. More remarkable still was the fact that these people were never sick with any serious illness.

They all—including my second uncle, the pharmacist—treated common illnesses with home remedies.

By Vilcabamba's longevity standards, my mother could also live a few more years, and I had hopes of helping her to regain her health. The first thing I had to do was eliminate all the medication. Following that, we would begin a detoxification diet.

The first two days were very rough for her because her system was addicted to the drugs. My being a nutritional consultant also was very important in providing her with the best diet for her condition. Other side effects from the drug given to her at the hospital were mouth sores and difficulty in swallowing. She struggled with these problems for several days.

Before my trip to see my mother, I had prepared a mixture of amaranth, spelt, quinoa, and oatmeal flour, all organic, to take with me. All of these stone-ground, organic grains are high in fiber and a good source of protein. In addition, they contain no cholesterol and are low in calories, and because of her diabetes, they were good for her.

Her diet was a healthy one. For breakfast on the first day, she had a bowl of the organic, cooked flour mixture with grated apple and one teaspoon of Ensure drink for complete, balanced nutrition to help her with bodily weakness. For lunch, she was on a liquid diet consisting of homemade, organic chicken soup with almost no salt and very mild fresh herbs and spices, including rosemary, sage, and parsley. For the evening meal, she took a cup of mixed-herb tea with a slice of whole wheat, homemade, organic bread. She was given plenty of pure water to drink throughout the day.

The second day's menu was the same as the first day.

On the third day, she took the same breakfast, but for lunch, she had a small bowl of chicken soup, a very small portion of mashed potato with almost no salt, a piece of broiled chicken breast, and broccoli cut into small florets. For the evening meal, she took vegetable soup, a piece of whole wheat, homemade bread, and a cup of herb tea.

The herb tea was made with dandelion root to purify the kidneys and corn silk, a diuretic, to help cleanse the bladder and kidneys. There were other herbs from the vast array that are available in Ecuador, but I do not know their names in English. All are used in my country to detoxify the system.

On the fourth day, she took the same breakfast with B complex and fresh fruit juice. For lunch, she had organic brown rice, broiled fresh fish, and cooked spinach. For the evening meal, she took cream of broccoli soup and a small piece of whole wheat bread.

Since her bedroom was on the second floor, the second week, we made her walk slowly downstairs, because exercise is another key factor for healing. Walking is good for the heart and especially for type 2 diabetes. Exercise also helps to improve sleep patterns and get rid of stress, anxiety, and depression. She got used to walking, and every day, she would walk a little bit more.

By the fifth day, my mother had regained her complete sense of self, and she could recite her social security number with confidence. After three weeks, she went with my sister and me on a one-day trip to a tourist site. She enjoyed every minute of that trip.

My mother is still alive as of this writing, ninety-four years old.

The main factors in any person's healing are the elimination of chemicals, good nutrition, a deep sense of faith through prayer, and unconditional love, attention, and personal care. This nurtures not only the body but the mind and spirit as well.

# TWENTY-FOUR
## The Secret Life of the Unborn Child

I read through Thomas Verny's book, *The Secret Life of the Unborn Child*, for the first time while I was on vacation in Ecuador. I was staying in the Madre Tierra Resort and Spa in Vilcabamba, thirty kilometers from my hometown of Loja. From the first pages, I was enthralled. I used the jaw-dropping quote from Leonardo da Vinci to introduce this book. Here Verny has a bit more to say about him, and I will, too. All page numbers in parentheses without other information apply to this book (Verny 1981):

> The great Italian artist, inventor and genius . . . had more to say about prenatal influences than many of the most modern medical texts. In one especially insightful passage, he wrote: "The same soul governs the two bodies . . . The things desired by the mother are often found impressed on the child which the mother carries at the time of the desire . . . One will, one supreme desire, one fear that a mother has, or mental pain, has more power over the child than over the mother, since frequently the child loses its life thereby." ( 34)

Further checking while at work on this book reveals that Leonardo made this observation in two different sketchbooks (*Quaderni*). On page 8 of sketchbook 3, we find the desires of the mother being "engraved" (impressed) on the newborn. On page 10 of sketchbook 4, he talks about how the mother's wishes or desires are felt more powerfully, both emotionally and physically, by the child than the mother. Because the mother and child are in a stage of "oneness" during the gestation period, when the mother is exposed to negative news, for example, the negative emotion can cause a miscarriage, threatening the child's life and causing immediate harm to the mother. In both of Leonardo's quotes, he talks about "one soul" and the dying of the child by sudden fright.

It was thrilling to hear these ideas expressed more than five hundred years ago by a great man who didn't have my advantage in knowing how a mother feels when she is pregnant. Yet the "supreme desire" (also translated as an "intense desire") described by Leonardo went right to the heart of the matter. And what I thought of as one mind was clearly the "one soul" of da Vinci that governs and nourishes both mother and child.

Verny is acknowledged to be a pioneer in research dealing with neonatal and perinatal psychology, having taught at Harvard and York University (in Canada) and having practiced for years in Ontario. His book changed thinking in the twenty-seven countries where it was published. Yet it's hard to find today. Back in Texas, I had read Hawkins first because of the easy style, but here, I took my time with Verny.

I was very excited to find many of my thoughts and feelings in the book. The book leaves us with a huge respect for the sensitivities and responses of the unborn child. Line after line spoke to me directly, such as, "New research is also beginning to focus much more on the father's feelings . . . Studies . . . show that how a man feels about his wife and unborn child is one of the single most important factors in determining the success of a pregnancy" (13).

Later, the author goes further with the following bombshell: "During these months, the woman is her baby's conduit to the world. Everything that affects her affects him. And nothing affects her as deeply or hits with such lacerating impact as worries about her husband (or partner). Because of that, few things are more dangerous to a child emotionally and physically than a father who abuses or neglects his pregnant wife. Virtually everyone who has studied the expectant father's role—and sadly, so far, only a handful of researchers have—has found that his support is absolutely essential to her and, thus, to her child's wellbeing" (30).

Well, my pregnancy had been an undoubted success in producing a truly beautiful and genetically well-endowed human being. From my child's point of view, nothing bad had ever happened to her. There was nothing wrong with the world as she found it. What was evil and upsetting in it was coming from other people—ignorant people, misinformed people . . . and if I were to be completely honest with myself, I had to acknowledge that I had once been one of them.

Verny's ideas and all the research he draws upon "forever displaces the old Freudian notion that personality does not begin forming until the second or third year" (16). No wonder my studies in classical psychology had gone nowhere. "Unlike givens such as genetic inheritance, [maternal thoughts and feelings] . . . are controllable. *A woman can make them as positive a force as she wishes*" (16). If only I had understood this years ago!

Furthermore, "Dr. Michael Lieberman showed that an unborn child grows emotionally agitated (as measured by the quickening of his heartbeat) each time his mother thinks of having a cigarette. She doesn't even have to put it to her lips or light a match; just her *idea* of having a cigarette is enough to upset him" (20).

How could basic research like this escape the attention of people trying to understand homosexuality and gender identity issues? How could so many children be blamed for their problems with gender identity when such a clear basis for it could be so easily proven? Now more than ever, I sensed that I'd found some of the answers in all my reading, but they needed to be applied to what Verny was saying back in 1981. And pregnant women's feelings were still not being taken into account in what was being written today.

The currents of my own life were coming together. I'd had a sense that homosexuals and people with gender identity issues had been left out because the people doing the research and teaching courses—overwhelmingly male, by the way, as they were in Candace Pert's day—were not interested in trying to find a reason for LGBTQ issues that would put so many people out of work. I'd had the same revelation when I began to understand that the stress that causes most cancer couldn't be treated with medication, chemotherapy, or radiation, but could be treated by getting rid of stressors residing in our minds and spirits. Our highly technological society is deeply engaged in solving problems of its own making. Our people are being tantalized by breakthroughs of one kind or another, but too many leaders in our churches and schools and too many politicians and social workers want to take sides as to the correct way to deal with problems.

How could so many people be looking the other way when the evidence was in that a lot of cancer therapy was making things worse for those being treated? A vast number of people dealing with the "problem" of homosexuality wanted all the responsibility for it to lay with LGBTQ people themselves, with the unenlightened people on one side who didn't understand all the therapy and research, or with the unenlightened people on the other side who were invested in their own complex understanding of the matter and who—perhaps unintentionally—were preventing people from taking responsibility for the kind of life their children would enjoy.

Methods to reduce the stress we face in life were available to all of us at no cost. Knowledge about the way parents could influence their unborn children could become common knowledge just as easily, and there would be far fewer problems to solve.

Because of Verny's openness and thoroughness when going into so many issues involving parental influences and fetal development, I was with him every step of the way. Since I'd been thinking about these issues for many years already, I recognized my own experiences in almost everything he was saying. But because I've also said so much about my pregnancy and the reasons for my thinking about it, I feel it would burden the reader to hear all the ways that Verny's ideas and findings corresponded to my own.

Never was there any direct correlation between parental desires and homosexuality and gender identity differences, but this was something that I now felt able to explain—a story waiting to be told.

I read every word in the book, and, as soon as I turned the last page, I went back to the beginning and read everything again. I felt connected to a lot of information from the recent past and even from the distant past that was being ignored. And I felt like a living connection between the women who had told me their feelings when they were pregnant and people like Dyer, Weil, Sarno, McTaggart, Lipton, Pert, Hawkins, and now Verny, all of whom had taught me so much.

Although I was still far from being able to put my ideas in a book and find readers for such a book, I was on my way. I have never had difficulty following a path. I have never been easily frightened by the new places it has taken me and the sometimes surprising or disturbing conclusions I have been forced to make. I know that I have what Americans call "grit," and knowing this, I was sure that, someday, I would be able to do something to ease the burden of LGBTQ children who are born with gender issues and are treated unfairly all their lives, even as children, for expressing themselves in a way that is totally natural for them. It may have been too late for me to change any of the particular occurrences in my own family, but I knew my daughter well enough to realize that she would respect me for what I was doing, even though the work and the good I might be able to do would do nothing to make things easier for her.

As my daughter was a big-hearted person who revealed her noble nature as an infant and seemed to grow in stature the rest of her life, I knew she would be proud of my work and deeply sympathetic with my desire to correct the wrongs of my youth. If I know her at all, I know that she is grateful for good wherever she finds it, and she has strength enough to shrug off things that cause her pain and move on. So, of course, every word of this book is motivated by my love for her. The more I think about her life, the more I realize the depth of that love.

# CONCLUSION
## My Daughter's Story

*"My mother, the leading lady in my life; my rock, my inspiration, to whom I owe everything I am . . . I love her."* (My Valentine's Day message to my mother, February 14, 2015.)

Those who know me know how very proud my mother has made me over the years because of her relentless refusal to accept a life of despair and failure. Those who've read her book don't need me to tell them the kinds of challenges she faced. It would have been so easy to fall into those pits over and over again, but she was up to all the challenges that came her way.

In my own life, I've seen my share of middle-aged mothers, young mothers and fathers, and friends who have given up in the face of adversity. And I've known parents with the minds of children and friends of mine who've commented that now that they're in their midtwenties, they see how they've surpassed their parents in maturity and in their understanding of the world and find themselves acting like adults to their own parents (whether it be through financial support, emotional support, or both).

My case is different. As I've said many times, my mother has always been my rock. There is nothing she has ever promised and failed to deliver. I can see that I was probably spoiled in a way and expect a high standard from everyone I meet. I expect people to say what they mean, mean what they say, and deliver. I look for the thoughtfulness that my mother always showed me in all my friendships and relationships. She was in my room at six in the morning every birthday with a present, a cake, or playing my toy piano to wake me up to her birthday singing performance. I was picked up from school with a birthday card, and, sometimes, our house was full of friends who were waiting for me to start the celebration. I have never seen such perfection in the execution of love through action.

I've had peers and acquaintances who have told me their parents forgot it was their birthday or who had separated parents who never called them. And certainly they would never expect a card in the mail . . . It breaks my heart to think of the amount of love I have been given and to think that families, parents, children, brothers, and sisters could grow up in a less loving and sometimes loveless environment. I never knew that kind of sadness.

As a child, I liked to play with boys because I enjoyed physical activities and excelled in sports—all sports. The typical girls wanted to be in their rooms playing house, pretending to cook, clean, and mimic housework. I found all that completely boring compared to riding a bike, roller-skating, or playing catch or baseball. Maybe that's the reason why even at an elementary school age, I could directly compete with boys and was outperforming the average girl.

Many girls couldn't even throw a ball in the right direction, which was frustrating to me when I was so competitive by nature and wanted to win and excel at everything I did. Maybe this is what's called "nature and nurture." My mother was always reassuring me and leading by example to create and invent when there was need. If I practiced and work hard, there were no limits to what I could achieve. In a sense, I didn't allow my sex to be an obstacle or allow myself to be locked into what is "only for girls."

As regards my upbringing, homosexuality, gender identity "disorder," and dysphoria are terms I don't identify with. My own view of myself is much simpler: I am just me. It is my understanding that there is not supposed to be anyone else like me. I truly fail to understand why the world has to be divided into a finite number of categories and people have to possess the same traits. The term "disorder" offends me and doesn't identify me in any way.

There's nothing wrong with my mind, body, or being. Since I was born with a deviated septum, I guess I can say I do have one deformity! But how can LGBTQ identity be such a touchy and delicate situation? If LGBTQ identities have and always will be present, why do I get a completely different feeling from hearing that term than from having a CT scan and being told once and for all, "Your septum is deviated." As I see it, LGBTQ identities have been handled in many mistaken ways or not handled at all. Why can't LGBTQ identities be looked at in the same factual and underwhelming way a doctor would diagnose anything else?

My hope for this book is to press out into the forefront and continue the journey of proving the normalcy of LGBTQ people and the idea that people simply are who they are; they are your friends, coworkers, leaders, servants, peers, neighbors, and sometimes your own family members. Why would anyone focus on causing division and separation because of the love or sexual preference or tendencies of another human being? Why would the love one person shares with another cause a third person's hatred or intolerance?

Above all else, I believe in love, and where love is present, permanent division or discord cannot survive; that is why I am certain that, though it will take time, the LGBTQ group will one day achieve equality. Love and acceptance will prevail.

I had no intention of telling my mother I was attracted to females until the day I was certain I had met "the one." I had my first relationship at nineteen, living out on my own in a big city. It had also been quite a process for me. As far as I knew, I had always been heterosexual because I knew no other way of life, despite a few conversations I imagine most teens have with their friends while playing truth-or-dare games at sleepovers.

In a sense, a whole new world had opened up for me; in another sense, I was so comfortable in it that it was as if I hadn't skipped a beat and that nothing had changed for me or changed within me at all. I actually felt so unnaturally normal and unchanged that it was strange!

I told my mother at the age of twenty-two that I was attracted to females because I had gotten to a point where I felt she didn't really, truly know my life and that I had been hiding part of it from her by just not telling her the details. And I wanted to be close to my mother and for her to know the truth. The separation was getting to me, and I wanted to be able to talk to my parent as any child does when there is love, heartbreak, or advice that needs to be sought.

Of course, I was afraid of how she would take it. I did not want to hurt her, and I did not want her to blame herself or anyone else; most of all, I was scared she would denounce me for the way I was living or wanted to live. I was afraid my future was about to change drastically and that I would lose my family, all the love that I had been spoiled with, and the emotional support I had always counted on in my endeavors.

Looking at statistics and remembering the fear I felt just moments before saying what could have been life-altering words—some of the most life-altering words I had ever spoken—I understand firsthand the fear of LGBTQ people who don't want anything to change with their loved ones.

To think that this form of love between people isn't being recognized and revered in a world filled with hate and death and turmoil is, to me, a sin. Love is fluid in nature. Sometimes, it exists as a means to an end; sometimes, it is meant to flow freely; sometimes, to love is simply good in itself. It's a completely selfless act in which we are the channels through which it flows, and that's all there is to it. We must be vessels of love operating in love.

Throughout my adulthood and professional career, I can honestly say that I have never been directly discriminated against because of my sexuality, at least, not that I know of. Of course, I do not parade my sexual preferences in any setting, but if appropriate or if asked, I'm a very open person, willing to talk to anyone about anything. I can't say I'm terribly shy about too much. We all have embarrassing moments— moments of wardrobe malfunctions, moments of absolute horror, like walking out of the restroom with two feet of toilet paper hanging from the back of your pants and the luck of having your crush notice it before anyone else . . . Ugh . . . It's all so awful, and it's all so human.

As I've grown from all my experiences, I've come to realize that we are all different, but so many of us can relate to the same basic human emotions and needs, such as sharing in laughter, hunger, necessity, sadness, adversity, and happiness. I realized that the goal should be to become the best versions of ourselves that we can be: this has been one of my truths in early adulthood. I shouldn't try to be like anyone else because that would mean ignoring my own skills and abilities and trying to function through someone else's. Oscar Wilde said it best: "Be yourself; everyone else is already taken." Ignoring what my Creator made me seems like an insult, as if He made a mistake and as if I am not grateful for what I am and the gifts and talents He has given me.

In church, I used to hear to lay down your flesh, let go of your earthly desires, do not let success and riches guide you in this world. Then I remember reading *The Fountainhead* by Ayn Rand. One quote has never left me: "And no one came to say that your life is your own and the good is to live it." *Wow*, I thought, *that seems sacrilegious in a way and like the Antichrist's teaching.*

But what if it were OK to accept our humanness? Continuing to strive for spiritual awakening, of course, but what if our desires are not all sinful? Would the waste not be the underutilization of the gifts, talents, and strengths we've been equipped with? Would this not be a form of sin, and a grave sin, to basically say that I won't use what I have? That I choose to ignore the riches and skills He has bestowed upon me?

There are several contexts in which I feel either comment is possible, but at what point do you say, "I'm going to give away everything earthly I have and be homeless in the pursuit of spiritual righteousness"? What is the limit there? Pushing Ayn Rand's statement to the extreme, can I live a life that benefits me and me only—a life of riches, of gluttony and excess, of not caring how I will affect those around me?

It seems to me that the quote from Ayn Rand is a completely different take on the usual religious message of self-abandonment. Perhaps there can be a balance between the two. Perhaps a life of self-love and righteousness can exist alongside a life of giving.

I have never settled for being average or for being what's tolerable or acceptable for a female to be. I have always had this mix of both the masculine and the feminine in me, whereby I naturally strove to compete with the best, male or female. The best is the best, right? I never limited myself to categorization: "I AM this; therefore, I can only do THESE things."

Luckily, I was raised by wonder women (my mother and sister); they were role models for me not because of their own choices or physical strength but because of the things they had to do in order to survive. In this kind of situation, environmental influences are simplified, and it's easier to keep one goal in mind: to survive. For me, surviving became thriving, a graduation of the momentum I'd acquired, and there was a continuation to success at the same speed. As I remember reading, we put up our own boundaries. If we do not accept the expected or the merely tolerable, then breakthroughs, change, and progress are inevitable. All that's required of us is relentlessness.

# References

A.D.A.M., Inc. 2015. "Gender Identity Disorder." Health Guide, *New York Times*, April 3. http://www.nytimes.com/health/guides/disease/gender-identity-disorder/overview.html.

Angell, Marcia. 2004. *The Truth about the Drug Companies: How They Deceive Us and What to Do about It*. New York: Random House.

Chopra, Deepak. 1989. *Quantum Healing: Exploring the Frontiers of Mind/Body Medicine*. New York: Bantam.

Dyer, Wayne W. 2005. *The Power of Intention*. Carlsbad, CA: Hay House.

Fédération Cynologique Internationale. "FCI Breeds Nomenclature." http://www.fci.be/en/Nomenclature/.

Gates, Gary J., and Frank Newport. 2012. *Gallup Special Report: The U.S. Adult LGBT Population*. The Williams Institute, http://williamsinstitute.law.ucla.edu/research/census-lgbt-demographics-studies/gallup-special-report-18oct-2012/.

Hawkins, David R. 2012. *Power vs. Force: The Hidden Determinants of Human Behavior*. Carlsbad, CA: Hay House.

Healing Cancer Naturally. 2015. "Why Alternative Cancer Treatment." http://www.healingcancernaturally.com.

Holden, C. 2003. "Future Brightening for Depression Treatments." Science 31 (302): 810–13.

Holford, Patrick. 1997. *The Optimum Nutrition Bible.* Berkeley: Crossing Press.

Leaf, Alexander. 1973. "Every Day Is a Gift When You Are Over 100." *National Geographic* 143 (1): 93–119.

Lipton, Bruce. 2005. *The Biology of Belief.* Santa Rosa: Mountain of Love / Elite Books.

McTaggart, Lynne. 2008. *The Field: The Quest for the Secret Force of the Universe.* New York: Harper Perennial.

Online Medicine Tips. 2012. "Can Stress Cause a Fever?" http://www.onlinemedicinetips.com/privacy.html.

Peale, Norman Vincent. 2003. *The Power of Positive Thinking.* New York: Touchstone.

Pert, Candace B. 1997. *Molecules of Emotion: The Science Behind Mind-Body Medicine.* New York: Scribner.

Sahley, Billie J. 1995. *Chronic Emotional Fatigue: Why It Affects Your Mind and Body . . . How You Can Stop It!* San Antonio: Pain & Stress Center Publications.

Sarno, John. 1986. *Mind Over Back Pain.* New York: Berkley Books.

Seelke, Clare Ribando. 2008. *Ecuador: Political and Economic Situation and U.S. Relations.* Congressional Research Service, http://fas.org/sgp/crs/row/RS21687.pdf.

Silverman, Michael I. 2006. "Men with Older Brothers More Likely to be Gay." ABC News, June 26. http://www.abcnews.go.com/health/story?id=2120218.

teleSUR. 2015. "1.5 Million Lifted Out of Poverty in Ecuador under Correa." January 25. http://www.telesurtv.net/english/news/1.5M-Lifted-Out-of-Poverty-in-Ecuador-under-Correa-20150125-0019.html.

Trivieri, Larry, and John W. Anderson, eds. 2002. *Alternative Medicine: The Definitive Guide*. 2nd ed. Berkeley: Celestial Arts.

U.S. Cancer Statistics Working Group. 2014. *United States Cancer Statistics: 1999–2011 Incidence and Mortality Web-based Report*. Atlanta: U.S. Department of Health and Human Services, Centers for Disease Control and Prevention and National Cancer Institute. www.cdc.gov/uscs.

Verny, Thomas, with John Kelly. 1981. *The Secret Life of the Unborn Child*. New York: Dell Publishing.

Washington Apple Commission. 2010. "Apple Varieties." http://www.bestapples.com/varieties.

Weil Andrew. 1995. *Spontaneous Healing*. New York: Alfred A. Knopf.

*Wikipedia*. 2015. "Hummingbird." Wikimedia Foundation, Inc., August 3. http://www.en.wikipedia.org/wiki/hummingbird.

# ABOUT THE AUTHOR

G. M. Walser is a retired public accountant in commerce and business administration with forty-five years of business experience. Throughout her business career, she was the owner and manager of three successful businesses.

Also a painter born with artistic talent, Walser has many years of experience in natural and intuitive healing. She trained in natural medicine, received certification as a nutritional consultant and master herbalist, and earned a bachelor's of science degree in holistic health.

For more than twenty-six years of her life, Walser executed a private research study seeking answers to her intuition. She started this most difficult quest for truth in order to unravel and solve the mystery and the origin of homosexuality and gender identity.